*Get Through Everything
and Overcome Anything
with Water-Walking Faith in God.*

the WOW
ZONE

Series

WALKING ON WATER
when the ground ain't enuf

the WOW ZONE

Series

You unlock this door with the key of faith.
Beyond it is another dimension.
A dimension of grace.
A dimension of trust.
A dimension of favor.
You're moving into a land of both
hope and substance, of things seen and unseen.
WELCOME,
you've crossed over into **THE WOW ZONE™**,
where walking on water is a way of life!

COME ON. GET YOUR FAITH WET.™

ACCLAIM FOR STANICE ANDERSON

"With God-fearing candor, Stanice leaves an indelible mark on one's soul." **Victoria Christopher Murray, Essence Bestseller Author**

"Stanice is real. When she speaks, she stands naked, sharing the beauty and the horror of her life. Her writing, full of heart and grace, is just the same." **Sharon Ewell Foster, Christy Award-Winning Author**

"Like its author, Walking on Water When The Ground Ain't Enuf, is authentic, uplifting and inspired reading for anyone needing the wind at their back for transportation to a special place." **S Robert Morgan, Actor/Director (played Butchie on HBO's The Wire)**

"Stanice Anderson is one of the most inspiring motivational speakers I know. She gives us the truth (in love, of course) and all of her books will spur you to action and boost your faith." **Carol M. Mackey, Author of Sistergirl Devotions**

"Stanice's words will make you soar above whatever is holding you down. Consider *Walking On Water When The Ground Ain't Enuf*, as a jet ski polished to an amazing shine by years of walking in faith. Open the book covers, hop on board, and get ready to get your feet wet." **Patrice Gaines, Author, Speaker & former Washington Post Reporter**

"A powerful speaker. An inspirational woman." **ZANE, Owner, Strebor Books**

"Stanice is an inspiring example of the power of perseverance, pushing through storms, and practicing prayer. Her water-walking faith will strengthen your own!" **Stacy Hawkins Adams Author & Speaker**

"If you want to learn how to mount up on wings like an eagle, or run and not get weary, start by watching Stanice walk on water!" **Joy Jones, Author/Playwright**

"Profoundly inspiring." **Booklist** (I Say A Prayer For Me)

"Stanice's story is so inspiring, real, and honest." **Amanda Gale, The 700 Club**

"Gripping...with a novelist's eye for dialogue..." **Publishers Weeky** (I Say A Prayer For Me)

"What Stanice has done is reconfigure her life, her triumphs and sorrow; through art in a way that takes us to unspeakable uplift." **Karen Evans, Black Women Playwrights' Group**

"Awesome watershed book to get you to speak to your mountains and watch them move!" **Pam Perry, Chief Visionary, Ministry Marketing Solutions**

"We can all learn wonderful and marvelous things from her powerful teachings within the pages of this book." **Barbara Joe Williams, Author**

She makes powerful parallels and connections to emotional and spiritual battles that all of us experience. We were led to tear off masks, dare to be real and transparent after spending time with Ms. Anderson." **Bernice Mayfield, Heritage Church**

We celebrated her creative brilliance & sassy stories of trauma and triumph. We laughed, ·cried, and embraced Stanice's journey as she reminded us to transcend our fears and get our feet wet, too." **Louise V. Gray, Publicist/Playwright**

"Ms. Anderson is a powerfully moving and uplifting speaker." **Anna Jones, Oxford House Inc., World Services Office**

"I love Stanice's *voice*, wit and wisdom. She's enormously talented with something important to say in a very entertaining way—so she makes you eager to hear it." **Pat Arnold, PhoeniX Productions**

"Maya Angelou's literary talent and Iyanla Vanzant's prayerful insights. Stanice knows the power of words, and moreover knows the power of love!"" **Sonsyrea Tate, Author**

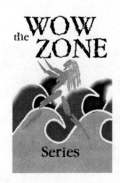

the WOW ZONE

Series

WALKING ON WATER
when the ground ain't enuf

STANICE ANDERSON

Shout Glory LLC

Washington, DC

Walking On Water when the ground ain't enuf
Published by Shout Glory LLC
Anacostia Station, P.O. Box 30430, Washington, DC 20030

For information regarding special discounts for bulk purchases, email
sales@TryWalkingOnWater.com.

Book the author as speaker, performance artist, or workshop facilitator for
your events. Also available for Skype™ Virtual Visits, and Speakerphone
Chats, contact booking@TryWalkingOnWater.com.

Visit www.TryWalkingOnWater.com

Printed in the United States of America
First Printing: November 2010   10 9 8 7 6 5 4 3 2 1

ISBN 978-0-615-33804-0 (pbk)   E-book also available
Library of Congress Control Number: 2010917541

1. Anderson, Stanice 2. Christian biography—United States 3. Title
4. Christian: Spiritual Growth 5. Christian Living

Executive Editor, Mike E. Tucker, Jr.
Cover Design and Layout, Mike E. Tucker, Jr.
Cover Painting by Demont"Peekaso" Pinder
Graphics Design by Denise Johnson
Interior Book Design by Stanice Anderson and Michal Zoe Tucker
Water-Walker Graphic Concept by Stanice Anderson

DEDICATION

This book is dedicated to the Water-Walkers
who show us that we can get through
everything and overcome anything
with water-walking faith in God.

IN MEMORY OF

TERESA SMITH HILL
CAROL LOVING POWERS

Water-Walkers, indeed!
Your lives indelibly impacted my life.
Love never dies.
You live in every word I write.

*"Lord, if it's you," Peter replied,
"tell me to come to you on the water."
"Come," he said.*

Matthew 14: 28-29, NIV

Also by Stanice Anderson

I SAY A PRAYER FOR ME
One Woman's Life of Faith and Triumph
(Walk Worthy Press/Warner Books)
soon-to-be re-published Shout Glory LLC edition)

12-STEP PROGRAMS
A Resource Guide For Helping Professionals
(Learning Publications)

(Contributing Author)
SISTAHFAITH
Real Stories of Pain, Truth and Triumph
(Howard Books/Simon & Shuster)

(One-Woman Show)
WALKING ON WATER WHEN THE GROUND AIN'T ENUF

(Speaker Tours)
GET THROUGH AND OVERCOME
WITH WATER-WALKING FAITH

LET'S GET REAL
SHARING OUR STORIES—SHARING OUR STRENGTHS

I AM MY SISTERS' KEEPER

CONTENTS

CONTENTS

CONTENTS

CONTENTS

Jesus and Peter Walk on the Water

^{22}*Immediately Jesus made the disciples get into the boat and go on ahead of him to the other side, while he dismissed the crowd.* ^{23}*After he had dismissed them, he went up on a mountainside by himself to pray. When evening came, he was there alone,* ^{24}*but the boat was already a considerable distance from land, buffeted by the waves because the wind was against it.*

^{25}*During the fourth watch of the night Jesus went out to them, walking on the lake.* ^{26}*When the disciples saw him walking on the lake, they were terrified. "It's a ghost", they said, and cried out in fear.*

^{27}*But Jesus immediately said to them: "Take courage! It is I. Don't be afraid."*

^{28}*"Lord, if it's you," Peter replied, "tell me to come to you on the water."*

^{29}*"Come," he said.*

Then Peter got down out of the boat, walked on the water and came toward Jesus. ^{30}*But when he saw the wind, he was afraid and, beginning to sink, cried out, "Lord, save me!"*

^{31}*Immediately Jesus reached out his hand and caught him. "You of little faith," he said, "why did you doubt?"*

Matthew 14:22-31 (New International Version)

"God does not give us overcoming life—
He gives us life as we overcome.
The strain of life is what builds our strength.
If there is no strain,
there will be no strength."

Oswald Chambers

WALKING ON WATER WHEN THE GROUND AIN'T ENUF

What am I doing?
I'm living so completely contradictory to what man says.
Mine is not a traditional life but only life as I've come to
know it.

A series of leaps of faith,
walks on water, climbs up mountaintops,
exiles to deserts, dodging the shadows of death in valleys
and refusing to be a Jesus cliché.

I'm walking on water when the ground ain't enuf!
Can you relate?

Every day I awake expecting miracles, favor and success
with God, people and institutions.
My bank account says "It's not happening."
The bills say, "You've got to be kiddin'. Debt-free?
We ain't having it."
The mortgage company says,
"Half-step one time…miss one beat!"

My past, dares me to step outside the box it build for me
as it reminds me of the mess I was
and the disappointment I will always be.

Some days my mind is not my friend.
But I'm tearing down the self-imposed walls today.
If not now when? If not me who?
Can you relate?
What am I doing?

I'm walking on water when the ground ain't enuf!
I'm not listening to the whispers of doubt anymore,
I don't care how loud they get or if they sing in six-part
harmony.

You're too old? You didn't go to the best schools, or
wear the flyest clothes.
Nobody wants to hear what you have to say.

Shut up, I say! Back up off me!
I'm not listening any more.
I'm not listening any more.
I'm walking on water when the ground ain't enuf!

What am I doing? I'm taking God at his word.
He said, *"For I know the plans I have for you; plans to
prosper you and not to harm you, plans to give you hope
and a future."*

My Helper, the Holy Spirit, encourages me
to call what is not as if it already is.
Empowers me to believe
that the impossible is highly probable
and that the possible is too easy for God anyway.

What am I doing?
I'm untying my boat from the shore.
I'm launching out in the deep waters.
I'm stepping out the boat with Jesus in my view.
I'm walking on water when the ground ain't enuf!
Can you relate?

From Stanice's One-Woman Show, *Walking On Water When The
Ground Ain't Enuf*, © 2007.

INTRODUCTION

You unlock this door with the key of faith. Beyond it is another dimension. A dimension of grace. A dimension of trust. A dimension of favor. You're moving into a land of both hope and substance, of things seen and unseen. You're about to cross over into the first book in the *The WOW Zone™* Series, **WALKING ON WATER WHEN THE GROUND AIN'T ENUF**.

WOW is the acronym for **W**alking **O**n **W**ater. Life in *The WOW Zone™* is a way of living that empowers you to get through everything and overcome anything with water-walking faith in God. It is synonymous with believing what God says in His Word to the point where acting on it becomes as vital as breathing.

This way of life we strive for is based on Matthew 14:22-31. It's the amazing story of Jesus, **naturally** so, walking on water. Empowered by Jesus' simple command, *"Come to me,"* Peter, by faith, steps out of the boat and **supernaturally** walks on the water toward Jesus.

Perhaps Peter was given the opportunity to empower his life, but God knew the story would be shared with us so that we, too, would come to believe that as regular, earthly people we can listen to that small still voice of Jesus in our hearts and step out of our own boats (comfort zones, if you will) and trust Him to enable us to exhibit the same faith as Peter. We, too, can walk on His waters to the glorious lives He preordained for us. And

xxiii

perhaps, in allowing us to see Peter's weaknesses as he took his eyes off Jesus and looked at the billowing waves around him, his faith wavered and he began to sink. But in not letting Peter sink, Jesus assures us that even when we take our eyes off of Him and get enveloped in the situation and circumstances that surround us, He'll be there for support. As Matthew 14:31 calls out from ages past, *"Immediately Jesus reached out his hand and caught him. 'You of little faith,' he said, 'why did you doubt?'"*

So this story is not just about potent, sacred words on a page but a living and breathing personal, intimate promise that speaks to our hearts and minds across the living waters of time. It is a new way of living, trusting and leaning on God through whatever life brings our way. We can use it to develop, grow, and live a life worthy of our calling as chosen ones—water-walkers!

So when you need a physical or emotional healing for yourself or loved ones, today, like spoken to His child, disciple and friend, Peter, Jesus says to us, *"Come to me."*

When you've been laid off, the unemployment benefits run out, and the job interviews are not turning into job offers as quickly as you hoped, listen to the still small voice, as Jesus invites, *"Come to me."*

When the bills multiply faster than roaches can scatter when you turn the lights on, stop and listen to the voice that taps gently on the door of your heart.

When you feel like a motherless child and friends forsake you, the voice is clear, if you're willing to shut out the whispers of doubt and the clamor of the world, you'll sense the Holy Spirit's whisper, *"Come to me."*

When you don't know where the tears end and the shower begins, cry out to God; He's waiting. He'll answer, in a still, quiet voice, *"Come, let's walk on the water, you and I."*

When you feel like you're too old to dream and it's too late to care, He knows it's your low-self esteem that speaks for you and still, the Creator of the universe and universes yet discovered, holds you high as His child and friend. Shhhh. He whispers, *"Come to me."*

When you're young and feel like no one cares for you or you've been in one unloving foster care or group home setting too many, or bullies taunt you to hide soul sicknesses of their own, Jesus seeks to remind you that He cares and encourages you, *"Come to me."*

When traumatic memories of your past get a chokehold on your todays and try to sabotage your future, He will say, *"Come to Me."*

When the *"I'll nevers"* outweigh the *"One day I wills,"* He pleads, *"Come to Me."*

When your life seems encrusted with dried mud and your back is against the proverbial wall, Jesus tenderly calls you by name and says, *"Come to me."*

After you've been tossed that last load of bricks that you hope won't break your spirit or your back, Jesus invites you, *"Come, all you who are heavy laden and I will give you rest. For my yoke is easy and my burdens light."*

When you feel lonely in your *perfect* marriage and alone with your *right* crowd; when you feel homeless in a mansion and poverty-stricken on your yacht, Jesus beseeches, *"Come let's walk on the water, you and I."*

After I've prayed, cried and snotted about whatever … after the visiting bishop and ministry team who laid hands on me and anointed my head with olive oil have left the building, do I trust God? After the makeup is off, the jewelry is on the dresser and I'm alone, faced with myself, no longer able to rely on myself, during those times I dared to trust God.

When there is no one who sees me but God, my testimony bears witness that because of God's grace, mercy, and love, I've become—through it all—woman enough to believe God. I've heard enough sermons, cried enough tears to know when to take God at His Word and untie my boat from the shore, launch out into the deep waters, step out of the boat and get my faith wet.

When in the stillness of the night, in your heart you sense His whisper saying, *"Come to me. Trust me,"* step out of the comfort zone of your boat into the *WOW Zone* where walking on water is a way of life.

As we follow Jesus, He will make us fishers of men, women and children. Our faith will take the steps for us and our testimonies will help us keep our eyes fixed on Jesus. And when we sometimes falter as we look and listen to the thrashing waves all around us, like with Peter, Jesus will reach out His Hand and catch us—pulling us safely back to the surface. And perhaps He will scold us—gently, *"You of little faith, why did you doubt?*

How The Book Works

This book is simple and heart-driven. It reads like an intimate conversation between friends. That was my intention. It is not linear or in chronological order. So feel free to jump in where you will and get your inspirational read on.

Because it is not linear, you don't have to read from beginning to end. You can pick any chapter and read in any order. Each chapter, with its first-person real stories from my life, testimonies, monologues, poems or what I call *spokentry* - which is a cross-pollination of poetry and spoken word - is self-contained with a life of its own. This can be of great benefit to those on-the-go, who want an inspirational read during a commute, a break between classes, or during your prayer and meditation time. It's a book that fits today's lifestyle.

Chapters are built on relevant scriptures and sealed with powerfully personal prayers.

Together, my hope is that you will be inspired, motivated, and encouraged in your life's journey toward an unwavering, water-walking faith that will get you through everything and help you overcome anything that might try to keep you from moving forever forward with the wonderful and marvelous plans that God has for your life.

My prayer is that within each of my written offerings, above all else, you will see God's love, grace and mercy, and be reminded that God says, *"I alone know the plans I have for your life; plans for prosperity and not disaster, plans to give you a future and a hope."* (Jeremiah 29:11-13)

God promised long before I completed any of my manuscripts that He would meet each reader within the pages. He's kept, and will continue, to keep His word.

I'd love to hear from you about your experiences with this book and how God met you within the pages of **WALKING ON WATER WHEN THE GROUND AIN'T ENUF**.

Email me at WaterWalker@TryWalkingOnWater.com or comment on my blog at www.TryWalkingOnWater.com. I'd love to interact with you through Twitter or Facebook - www.twitter.com/stanice; www.facebook.com/stanice.

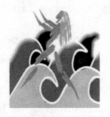

With water-walking faith,

the impossible is highly probable

and the possible is too easy for God anyway

CHAPTER 1: FAITH TESTIFIES

"And they overcame him by the blood of the Lamb,
and by the word of their testimony..."
Revelation 12:11 (NIV)

TELL ME A STORY

Tell Me A Story that I have not heard
Lead me to prayer; Give me an encouraging Word
Tell Me A Story that will teach me how to see
that God loves and cherishes even me

Tell Me A Story of God's Goodness and Power;
so I won't give up in this next hour
Tell Me A Story of what He's done for you; then maybe
I'll believe that He can do the same for me too
Sometimes I get weary. I get weak. I feel worn.
Tell Me A Story so I'll know it is not by mistake that I
was born

Tell Me A Story of how God leads the way
Tell Me A Story so that I can get through one more day
Tell Me A Story so I won't feel alone
Tell Me A Story of how faith is grown

Does God really work in mysterious ways?
Does God care how I spend the hours of my days?
Does He love me? Does He Care?
Will He always be there?
Tell Me A Story because sometimes life just ain't fair
Sometimes I feel like I'm living in a lion's lair

Tell Me A Story and please make it true
I need to know God loves me as much as He loves you.
Please Tell Me.

I Say A Prayer for Me: One Woman's Life of Faith and Triumph, (Walk Worthy Press/Warner Books), © 2002.

2

NOBODY TOLD ME THE ROAD WOULD BE EASY

There is one promise from God in the Bible that I've held onto like a lifesaving buoy in a swollen, wind-tossed sea. It anchors me and keeps me afloat. It compels me to look up and away from my sometimes overwhelming circumstances. It keeps my mind and heart locked on the hope that is breathed into every word. It's Jeremiah 29:11-13. *"God says, 'I alone know the plans that I have for your life, plans for prosperity and not disaster, plans to give you a future and a hope.'"*

Whatever has gone on or not gone on in my life, this promise helps me to know that nothing happens in my life that has not already been sifted through His hands.

I've been jobless, one pay check from homelessness, abandoned, lost loved ones to drug overdoses, domestic violence, AIDS, cancer, shootings and mental illness. I've been separated by miles and resentment from friends and lived many years without a vision for my life.

I've bled for months at a time while doctors tried to keep me alive until my health insurance kicked in and they could operate. Two husbands abandoned me and one was so abusive that I got a restraining order and had the sheriff take him away.

3

When I wanted to quit—I could not. When I wanted to give up—I dared not. When I laid dusty and tired by the side of the road and wanted with all that was left in me to go home and be with My Jesus—because life on Earth was so hard—I cried out with my hands held high toward the dark gathering clouds in my life, believing that despite my circumstances, it was not my time to die.

Only God could have poured that hope into me, stirred it around in my soul and charged to my rescue with His full regimen of ministering angels. What appeared to be my last stand became one of my greatest stands. A stand against the enemy that sought to torment my soul and seeks to kill, steal and destroy my faith and thwart the purposes God has for my life. After all, that is the enemy of my soul's job. But because *the one that is in me is greater than the one who is in the world,* I overcome. (1 John 4:4)

In the moments that I tap into the power of God, the words and music of that old song that the late Rev. James Cleveland sang with his deep, raspy voice, surge through my spirit. *"I don't feel no ways tired. I've come too far from where I started from. Nobody told me the road would be easy. I don't believe He brought me this far to leave me."*

Perhaps it appears dark in your life today. The shadows of emotional pain, too many bills, deferred dreams and dashed hopes are blotting out the sun around you and trying to crush your spirit. Maybe some days it feels like your weeping will never end and that your joy-in-the-morning-time will never come. But don't listen to lies or the whispers of doubt. All the promises that the Living God of the Bible makes, He never breaks.

Instead, take up the lamp of God—His Holy Word—and walk in the light that can chase the darkness from your path. In His presence darkness fades. Listen with your heart, linger in God's presence, let His promises permeate your soul and ignite your spirit to soar above the circumstances, despite what it looks like and what it feels like, to keep pace with what it always is—IN HIS HANDS. Know that the promises that the Living God of the Bible makes, He never breaks.

Find comfort and courage for the journey in knowing that the Maker of the Universe and everything in it loves you like you are the only one He has to love.

As further testimony, let's look at this book, ***WALKING ON WATER WHEN THE GROUND AIN'T ENUF***.

It seemed that the words begged to be written and released into the world. This book wouldn't take *wait* or *maybe* for an answer. When I insisted that we wait for my agent to shop it in the hope that it would be contracted by a New York publishing house, like my last book, *I Say A Prayer For Me*, everything inside me rose up with a resounding but inaudible, "No, that is NOT the route this time."

Slowly, it became clear that my brilliant and connected agent was unable to sell it. She offered me consolation through her professional knowledge of the volatility of today's market, which has hit everyone including the publishing houses. She took the time and gave me ideas on what the market could use and what I should write. Drop the non-fiction, write novels. Give the people what they want. But sometimes, perhaps like me, they don't know what they want until they see it, hear about it, see someone whose been changed by it and want it too. I can only write what I'm led to write at the time. Novels? Perhaps, later.

What does God want of me now? That was the question that was mine to ask and mine to wait for an answer. Though it tarried, I kept writing this manuscript, believing that it would be my next book.

One day, I felt led to approach a publisher friend on my own, and while she personally responded, "I love the title! I look forward to checking it out." She deemed my proposed book a little too new and risky for the times—and passed.

Still I believed, if I waited and held on, God would send me a publisher. It made perfect sense to me. He'd done it twice before; but as time passed and my manuscript neared completion, restlessness plagued me until one evening as I pondered, "*What now?*" A conversation I had years ago with my mentor, Dorine, replayed in my head like I was hearing it for the first time, *"Stanice, sometimes you can't go with the sensible. You've got to go with your heart and your gut feeling."*

I meditated on it. Sat with it for a while. The words of life lessons over two decades in the making: Sometimes, you can't go with the norm.

The truth in it grew louder and resonated within me. You can't go with what others say or do. Or what you think it should be. Sometimes you've got to swim against the current. Remember we walk by faith and not by sight. In tough and desperate times when your creativity begs to be birthed, loose the confines of the ground; stand up in your faith and walk atop the waves with your eyes focused on Jesus and all He has brought you through thus far.

There comes a time, after the last phone calls are made and the computer screen goes into hibernation mode, when the inner urgings of your spirit calls and you have to answer! On such a night, my spirit quivered as if touched by God, Himself, my mind and heart opened to a thought that before that moment either eluded me or in the noise of any ordinary day, I failed to recognize. Thoughts so pure I knew it could not be of an earthly origin, which is usually self-preserving, ambitious and selfish.

Now.

As I prepared myself to step up to the plate, a fast ball came out of left field in the form of a pink slip. Laid off from my job, I joined the ever-growing ranks of the unemployed. Couple the layoff with the necessity for double-knee surgery and it seemed like all hell had broken loose in my life. And just when I thought it was safe to get back in the water, my computer abruptly went to the dreaded blue screen, and then died. Everything I had ever written, including the manuscript for this book, was on the computer with no recent backup. How strategic that the attacks on my vision zeroed in on my finances, knees and computer. And while my computer could not be resurrected, an I.T. friend in California saved

7

my computer's soul—the hard drive. I walked on water—anyway. I wrote—anyway.

Assisted by family, friends, I gave inspirational talks, performed my one-woman show, assisted by friends and a cane that I put aside once I hit the stage. I determined, deep in my soul, to let nothing stop me from walking on water. Yes, I determined to let nothing take my focus off of Jesus. I wrote on. I walked on—in the Spirit.

But even with that kind of resolve, in the stillness of the night, when emotional and physical pain seems greatest, and a positive end seems to elude me, in those moments, I've wavered. Looking at the pain instead of focusing on the promise. Listening to the whispers of doubt, rather than Jesus' invitation, *"Come, let us walk on the water, you and I,"* which carries with it the power to enable me to do whatever He calls me to do.

Yet, **immediately**, like with Peter, he reached down—every time—and kept me from sinking.

Despite all of that and more, as far as this book project—STILL—everything inside me, shouted, *NOW!*

As my spirit leaped like a baby in a fertile womb, a string of words laced around my heart and formed sentences in my mind that seemed to come from the God of the universe:

Now is the time! Don't worry about the resources you don't have. Look to Me and know that you have every resource you will ever need in a thousand lifetimes at your disposal. Times are not just tough for you. There is nothing new under the sun and at this moment, like you, many are fearful of the unknown, disgusted and disappointed in the known, and hoping against all odds that they will triumph and get through these tough times.

People lost jobs today. Some lost loved ones. Today, people were diagnosed with illnesses or diseases and many were given prognoses that stung their psyches and crushed their hearts. Today, people received foreclosure notices. They purchased one-half of a prescription in order to get two-thirds of the groceries they needed. Today the retiree looked for work they need in order to make ends meet.

Today women were raped and children's lives and innocence were stolen.

For some, hope is dwindling as fast as a single mother's groceries.

Again, the words resonated within like sonar pings tracked on a submarine's monitor.

Now is the time! You can't wait until your life is a mirror of perfection and everything around you seems to point to a secure and easy time. That perfect time, my daughter, will only come when you are flowing in one accord with Me and my Holy Spirit. Write, gather, and pray over the pieces you have already written. While you're in the midst of getting through tough times, NOW is THE perfect time.

Thus, in faith, my son and I acted in faith and published this book that was destined to be— now.

Yes, these are tough times, indeed. But expect God to transform your mustard-seed faith into amazing, unshakable, immovable, unwavering, water-walking faith. Together, we will get through anything and overcome everything that tries to keep us from moving forever forward with the wonderful plans that God has for our lives. Perhaps, we triumph not in spite of it all, but because of it all.

Together, and with God being our Helper, we're walking on water when the ground ain't enuf—NOW!

THE HOUR I FIRST BELIEVED

One day Omie, my friend since childhood, quoted Revelation 12:11, "They overcame him by the blood of the Lamb and by the word of their testimony". She continued, "Stanice, God is going to use your experiences to free many people. Bookstores will have to open up a whole 'nother aisle for your writings–a testimony section." That was years before any of my books were published and years after God gave me a destiny-changing testimony.

♫ *Amazing grace, how sweet the sound,*
That saved a wretch like me.
I once was lost, but now am found,
Was blind, but now, I see. ♫

On some untraceable day, I crossed the imaginary line from recreational drug use to full-blown heroin addiction. Rejected by most of my family and friends, I lived alone and on the brink of eviction in an efficiency apartment. I cried often and in between sobs and self-pity, I stole, lied, schemed, and sold my body to supply my drug habit. I had an acquired soul sickness disease that my self-prescribed regimen of drugs no longer masked.

By the time I was thirty-five years old, every corner and crevice of my life hurt and I was convinced that it was too late to change. I existed in a constant state of hopelessness and despair. My spirit was dead and my body was tired of the vicious cycle and downward spiral of addiction—living to use and using to live.

I imagined myself dying on a bitterly cold night sprawled in a debris-strewn alley under a flickering street lamp as I foamed at the mouth like a rabid dog. I decided that a death as hard as my wretched life would be poetic justice.

Instead, alone in my bathroom one February evening, I stood in front of the mirror and injected a heroin/cocaine mixture into my hand and neck. Then, I walked through the living room toward the kitchen to get some Kool-Aid™. Before I got there, I heard a man's southern drawl-laced voice coming from my 13" black and white television. He talked of his heroin addiction and the consequences.

However, he also talked of grace.

Drawn to his words, I sat on my mattress on the floor in front of the TV. Buddy Baird was the name that flashed under his image. I wondered how my TV was tuned to The 700 Club. I never looked at that show for fear that it might provide God with a window into my life.

Although Buddy spoke of hopelessness, his elegantly chiseled white face, with half-parted lips that turned at the corners into a smile every time he said "But Jesus...," gleamed like a diamond under a noonday sun. He explained that he found a way out—or, rather, a way out found him.

I couldn't take my eyes off his handsome face. I yearned for the kind of peace and joy that resided in his eyes. Tired and disgusted with myself, it seemed like my soul shouted out, *"Talk to me, Buddy. Tell me what did you do? If you were where I am, how did you get out?"* I queried Buddy like he was in the room with me. I watched intently and waited for his answers.

In an instant the station switched from a live interview to a video reenactment of his story that was too much like mine. In one scene, Buddy stood by a window with a mirror and a heroin-filled syringe up to his neck as He searched for a willing vein. All of a sudden, it was not his image that I saw on the television screen—it was mine.

For the first time, I saw the unadulterated truth about what I had become—a desolate and addicted woman who desperately wanted to live but didn't know how. Like a carefully aimed laser in the skilled hands of a surgeon, Buddy Baird's story penetrated and disintegrated my thick wall of denial. Like a warm, melted healing salve, the message that he carried of Jesus' love, forgiveness, and power dripped into my aching soul.

However, there were old adages in my head that had been there so long that I believed them. Adages like, "you can't teach old dogs new tricks." Because of the way I lived as a heroin addict, I felt like an old dog. Another adage that weighed me down like a cord of logs tied around my neck: "You have to get your life right first and then go to God."

As if Buddy heard my thoughts he answered, "But Jesus came into my life and took my desire for drugs away. He changed me."

I wept as his words awakened my soul from a deep sleep and stirred my thoughts in a new direction, "Since Jesus changed Buddy's life, perhaps, He will do the same for me." With a child's heart, I seized the moment. Since I was already on the floor, I turned over onto my knees and prayed, "Jesus, help me. Do for me what you did for Buddy. Forgive me for my sins. I believe that you died for me and rose again. Come into my heart and live your life in me. Be my Lord and Savior. Amen."

Immediately, a strong sense of forgiveness and peace inflated my withered spirit like Wind in a flagging sail. I felt the burdens and sins of a lifetime whooshed away in a moment of sublime grace. A brilliant light flooded my apartment and I got up as if to welcome God into my life. Without thought, long-held secrets poured out of my heart and up through my lips. I uttered harm done to me and harm done by me. I confessed jealousies and resentments that were festering ulcers parasitically attached to my soul. Without trepidation, things that I dared not whisper in the dark, I exposed to God's light.

In the next moment, it felt as if I heard the Lord say, "I know. I saw you in the pigsty. I kept you alive through it all. I forgive you. You are preciously mine and I love you."

That frigid night in February turned out to be the warmest night of my life. I crossed over from hopelessness to hope and from death to life. Soon after, a pastor arranged my admission into an addiction treatment facility. I've enjoyed an intimate personal relationship with God through Jesus Christ and freedom from heroin addiction for over twenty-five years.

To think that the God of the universe came and walked with me, talked with me and told me I was His own—it's all too marvelous!

As a postscript, sixteen months after surrendering my life to Christ, The 700 Club sent a production crew to Washington, DC and videotaped a reenactment of my story. God also gave me the opportunity to be a guest on The 700 Club several times including a show where I met Buddy Baird. Together, we shared with a worldwide television audience how we overcame by the blood the Lamb and the word of our testimonies.

> ♫ *T'was grace that taught my heart to fear,*
> *And grace, my fears relieved;*
> *How precious did that grace appear*
> *The hour I first believed.* ♫

♫ Excerpt from hymn, Amazing Grace © Public Domain, Joseph M. Scriven, 1779

EVERYTHING TO GOD IN PRAYER

♫ What a friend we have in Jesus. ♫

Saved and on-fire for Jesus for a few months, I signed up for the methadone detoxification program operated by the government in an attempt to halt my heroin addiction. I drank my daily doses for months but I still nodded out in a now legal-drug-induced-stupor whenever I read my Bible. I allowed men to spend the night so that I had a guaranteed ride to the Methadone Clinic the next day. It soon became clear that my lifestyle hadn't changed even though I no longer used heroin.

♫ All my cares and grief to bear. ♫

So one day I prayed, "God, please get me off this methadone." The following day I went to the clinic and drank my usual dose of methadone. Within seconds, before I left the dispense counter, I had an allergic reaction that made me violently ill. My tongue swelled, my head pounded and I fell to the floor. The nurse yelled, "Call 911! Call 911!" Then there was my voice, muffled but audible, "Thank you, Jesus! Thank you, Jesus." Regardless of what I imagined it looked like to others, I knew that all was well. I knew that He heard my prayer and I was in the midst of His answer—life without methadone.

Days later, Reverend Kinard, then-Director of the Anacostia Museum and Assistant Pastor of the church I attended, across from the Methadone Center, arranged for my admission into an addictions treatment facility.

I didn't think I could stay clean for 24 hours; but on May 20, 2010, I celebrated 25 years clean and free from the bondage of active drug addiction—one day at a time.

♫ *What a privilege to carry everything to God in prayer!* ♫

Perhaps you are praying for someone, or praying for yourself, or not praying anymore because you are sick and tired of not seeing the results you want when you want them. How my parents must have not wanted to give up on me but felt they had to let me go because it was just too painful watching me kill myself on the installment plan.

How my son, must have wanted his momma in her right mind and in his life raising him like most of his friends mothers around him.

How my life barreled out of control with each toke, smoke, hit, drink, drop of a pill, or a syringe filled with warm heroin, with each change of town, men, outfits, that never filled the void in my soul—constantly changing seats on the Titanic but the ship was still going down! Then SUDDENLY, it seemed--EVERYTHING changed!

Hear this and be encouraged—as long as there is breath; there is hope. What God does for one, He will do for another.

My father saw me clean many years before he died in 1998. My mother and my son know firsthand that when it comes to God answering prayer—delay is not denial.

And I know—

♫ *Oh, what peace we often forfeit, Oh, what needless pain we bear, All because we do not carry everything to God in prayer.* ♫

♫ Verses excerpted from hymn, What A Friend We Have In Jesus © Public Domain, Joseph M. Scriven, 1855

I SAY A PRAYER FOR YOU

I stand with you in your prayers for peace, clarity, and provision! Today, I felt compelled to say a prayer for you.

DEAR HEAVENLY FATHER,

Please rebuke any and everything that is coming and trying to come against any and everyone who reads this. You know each one inside and out. You know the plans and promises that you have for each of our lives. Do for them what you did for me and more.

You didn't let the enemy steal my houses through threatened foreclosure—I sold them. You didn't let the enemy steal my joy—I cried sometimes but my underlying joy in You remained! You didn't let the enemy steal my mind or my life. You fought off the Hepatitis C and B viruses that the doctor said I had come in contact with in the past, and, as he put it, "your body fought it off." But I know who fought that battle and won!

Then, just last year, remember when my friends, Omie and her sister who is a nurse, insisted that I go in for a checkup even though I felt fine. I promised them I would, but somehow they sensed that I wouldn't. They insisted that I go the next morning and picked me up, drove me there, escorted me, and stayed with me in the waiting room. I complained the whole time about them treating me like a child.

19

When the nurse triaged me and took my pressure she called on you as she looked at me, "Oh, my God, Ms. Anderson, you are in stroke mode. Your pressure is 170/110."

I felt the tears spilling over my eyelids and I whispered, "Thank you, Jesus; you saved my life—again". The doctor attended to me and changed my medication.

I thank you, Lord for the gift of friendship and friends that may not tell you what you want to hear; but what you need to hear. Thank You for friends who take it a step further and act on your behalf; simply because they are compelled by The Holy Spirit. Yes, you are the Triune God in three persons.

I'm just sharing my testimonies as I pray, Lord, because I know that what You do for one you will do for another.

Father God, there are people going through financial difficulties beyond what they thought possible in one lifetime. I feel them. You remember God, how I woke up that morning not too long ago and thought my car had been stolen and called the police, only to find out that it had been repossessed. In time though, you gave me the means to buy another and even better car—with cash. Thus, paid in full; no car note.

And now once again, I find myself in the valley; but You remind me that flowers grow in the valleys; not on mountaintops. And from here, still I rise. Help my friends rise too, above and beyond what the world and the enemy of our souls would have us believe—that it will never be over and it's too late. Help us to recognize the lie from the father of lies. As long as there is breath— there is HOPE and our hope is in YOU.

Grant us Your peace that transcends all understanding. Grant us clarity so that we might see that nothing happens that is not sifted through your hands and You already made provision long before the trial even gets to our doors.

Thank You, now, on the front side, for what You are doing and about to do for us. Turn our situations around in an instant as we let go and let You do what You do so well—love and take care of us. We await the rewards of the faithful. For real, I'd rather be in a food stamp line with You than in a palatial home on the shore without You. I ask this in Jesus' Matchless Name. Amen. So be it!

CHAPTER 2: FAITH PURIFIES

"When you pass through the waters,
I will be with you;
and when you pass through the rivers,
they will not sweep over you.
When you walk through the fire,
you will not be burned;
the flames will not set you ablaze."
Isaiah 43:2 (NIV)

BEAUTY DESIGNED BY GOD

What do you dare to see?
I see the diamond dust glint about the eyes.
Even my soul feels warm and my dreams run deep.

Look at that strength in the jaw line, the sureness in the
step that dares to walk by faith where angels fear to tread.
I am a beautiful and blessed woman designed by God.

Mirror, Mirror on the wall, I see Beauty after all.

I see the two-sugars- one-cream coffee-colored face
tempered by time and softened by many salty tears
offered like sacrifices in the stillness of nights
 after the make-up is off and the jewelry is on the dresser
and there was no one at my side but God.

During such nights a humbled woman slowly emerged
healed and free from the muck and the mess. Beautifully
wrapped in the rich royal rainbow-colored robe of grace;
handcrafted by an unseen God who rescued me not a
minute too soon or a moment too late.

And now even when I'm real quiet and still, it feels like I
am dancing in a vast, freshly-cut field. With my head to
the sky, I bask in the warmth of God's light as it heals the
old and newly broken places in my life in my heart.

It's like I'm dancing—undisturbed—on Holy Ground.
Yes, I'm dancing undisturbed on Holy Ground.

FIRST THINGS FIRST

"Stanice, you've got mail," the husky baritone voice announced from my computer.

Ignoring my virtual assistant, I headed down the hall barefooted on the chilly hardwood floor towards the kitchen. First things first. Coffee.

I loved the aroma of freshly ground coffee wafting from my grinder signaling the beginning of a new day. From down the hall, I heard the husky voice again, "Stanice, reminding you is what I live to do."

"Yeah, yeah...I'm coming," I said between sips of coffee, as I walked back to my home office.

I sat down in my black ergonomic meshed high-back chair at my computer and offered up a quick prayer, "Lord, what would you have me do today?"

As I clicked the computer's mouse, the dark screen burst out of sleep mode and maximized my email inbox. The first unread email in line was from a sender whose named I recognized as a woman who was born again only a few weeks prior.

The subject line read, "Lost."

Without reading the body of the email, I thought I should have a little talk with God first. "Lost? Come on, Lord. Not today. I'm not ready for ministry. Give me some light stuff. I got a client's website to finish building—that I can do. Let me get lost in code and protocol. No? Then, how about the play? I can work on the script."

Either I wasn't getting through or I had not presented my case effectively, yet. While there was a tug at my heart to surrender, I continued, "Lord, you know that it's barely been three days since my traumatic experience. You remember!"

In my mind, I replayed the event of three days prior. It was Saturday 2:15 a.m., my car snuggly parked in front of my condo's window. When I woke up at 6:20 a.m., and looked out my window, the parking space was empty. My car was gone. Not wanting to panic, I prayed for composure and guidance, telephoned my son, and then the police. I prayed again and waited."

Later that day the police officer called back. "Ms. Anderson, I have news!"

"Great," I said, hoping that they recovered my car, and if not, no problem. I would make arrangements for a rental car through my insurance company.

He continued, "After putting your car into our nationwide computer system that I told you about earlier..."

"Yes, Officer?" Anxious, I couldn't wait for the man to swallow and get on with his next words.

"Ms. Anderson, your car was not stolen." He paused and then continued, "It was repossessed."

Now it was my time to swallow...and be silent. Swallow and be silent...swallow...

"Ms. Anderson, are you there?"

"Yes, Officer." I'm sure he said something else, but everything else was muffled as my brain strained to comprehend what I heard..."It was repossessed."

I answered him, "Okay. Thanks. Bye."

"Stanice, you've got mail," my virtual personal assistant's voice brought me back to my freshly brewed coffee and the fact that the day was going forward with or without my participation.

I took time to reflect on what I had experienced in the days since the car was taken. I thought about the praying, praising, being prayed over and prophesied to by my sisters in Christ, being encouraged and supported by my son, and feasting on God's Word. In the next moment, I made my choice-I prayed.

Father God, the repo man took possession of a car that evidently is no longer mine. I choose to believe that in answer to my prayer months ago, to tie up loose ends and remove financial burdens, I am now free from a car that felt like a one-ton boulder tied to my back with barbed wire. Keeping that car on the road interfered with priorities like shelter and food. I see this as a test of my faith and integrity that I will pass. I believe that I am on the verge of a major, long-awaited breakthrough and I can't turn around now.

Therefore, I stand on your promise that You alone know the plans you have for my life, plans for prosperity and not disaster, plans to give me a future and a hope. In Jesus' Name. Amen. So be it.

With my next breath, self-will ended. Purpose called me into that day. Determined to answer, I read my new acquaintance's entire email.

Subject: Lost. "Stanice, it has been almost one month since I have been saved and I am more confused than ever. Why can't I seem to get it right???"

I prayed for wisdom and responded. Subject: Found. "All is well with your soul. You are where each of us who love the Lord has been." I took a few sips of my now cooled coffee and continued tapping the words out from heart to the keyboard.

Perhaps you are going through a difficult time in your life. Something that makes you feel like you can't help anybody else. Like me, sometimes, you feel like, 'It's all about me, right now.' But as the Lord is teaching me–it's not all about me. It's about Him."

I don't believe that this mindset comes without a struggle. It's not natural to surrender, yield, or obey. It's against human nature. But, supernaturally, with God all things are possible; including desiring God's will more than our own.

Many of us are going through a faith-testing season, right now. I believe that the Lord reminds us what He said to Simon in Luke 22:30-32, as if He is saying to us now, "Simon, Simon, Satan has asked to sift you as wheat. But I have prayed for you, Simon, that your faith may not fail. And when you have turned back, strengthen your brothers."

And how do we overcome? God's word in Revelations 12:11 says, "They overcame him by the blood of the Lamb and by the word of their testimony; they did not love their lives so much as to shrink from death".

So no wonder the enemy of our souls, who also knows the Word, attempts to steal, kill, or destroy our relationship with the Savior of our Souls and our testimony. This is how we overcome. Both are our personal witnesses that GOD IS and forever WILL BE.

So what did I share with the new believer who God sent me via email? The Lamb of God and my testimony. I had been where she was and can be there again. I shared that I remembered one tearful night when I wrote in my journal, "God, it has been 21 years since you saved me and yet I am more confused than ever! Why can't I get it right?"

Now is the time for us to get real with ourselves and each other. Time is short and the harvest is ripe.

I thank God for my friend, Omie, who always says, "You got to read into everything using spiritual eyes."

The enemy of my soul knows that if he or his cohorts could have gotten me all yoked up about the car, concentrating on myself, operating in the *why me? why now?* mode, I would not have overcome. I would not have a testimony or an effective, spirit-filled ministry.

Living for and lusting after the things of this world—never satisfies. These things can take us OUT of the realm of ministry and instead banish us to an ever deepening, dank, and lonely hole called *ME-nistry.*

We must not forget that it's about the ministry. It's about lifting Jesus up—not ourselves—so that He can draw and make fishers of men, women and children who will hear His call and answer, "Yes, Lord, send me, too."

Hear Him knocking on the door of your heart; open it and say, "Yes, Lord, please come in and teach me wonderful and marvelous things I know nothing about. Please, live your life in me Sunday through Saturday."

INTO EACH LIFE
A LITTLE DUDE MUST FALL

Dude Duckett!
6 feet 5, caramel-brown skin with steel grey eyes.
13 years my junior.
Stole my heart at first glance.

All I saw was a scorching hot mid-life crisis romance.
It was about time.
I had my wait-time
beyond any wait that seems humanly possible.

But when Dude Duckett pulled his S-U-V over to the side
of the r-o-a-d,
Leaned over and grasped my hand,
Dude declared boldly,
        "Baby, I'm your Boaz. Your kinsmen redeemer!"

Say what? I wanted an instant replay.
Thank you, Jesus!
Finally, my black knight in slightly dull, off-white armor.

A month later, Dude Duckett, my kinsmen redeemer,
proposed.

Sold! Sign me up. And we were married.

After the honeymoon, Mr. Dude Duckett changed or had I
overlooked what I refused to see before I said, "I do?"

Which clothed in my right mind would have led me to
say, I don't so I won't.

But the voice, height, honey-dipped words, and the
infectious smile
camouflaged an anger management problem
laced with a tinge of unresolved resentments
topped off with a smidgeon of unbridled rage
exacerbated by mourning
the too recent death of his crack habit
and his insistence that wine and weed wouldn't lead him
back
to the same gigantic hole he dug for himself the last time.
And try to take me with him.

Like mountain hikers roped to each other waiting for an
avalanche
that my real Boaz and kinsmen redeemer, Jesus,
Already rescued me from years ago.

Don't you know,
Social worker blood runs through my veins,
Sometimes alluding my brain
I wanted to save Dude Duckett,
but instead I prayed for his removal.

Two days later,
Dude Duckett announced he wanted out of the marriage,
packed his clothes, yanked his Miles Davis limited edition
print off the wall
and left.

Nine months later,

CHAPTER 2: FAITH PURIFIES

Our divorce finalized,
He announced with the jubilance of a newlywed,
"I'm remarried with a three-month old son, isn't that cool?"

At that moment the pain of a love lost died an extremely joyful death.

I realized that I'd been saved from myself
and the Boaz-wanna-be.

Remind me to remember
Sometimes, the devil poses as an angel of light.

WHAT GOES AROUND

Somewhere along the line, unbeknownst to me,
the words twisted and turned against my husband
as he held me an emotional captive by words that only
hurt and hindered.

But I understand now.
I've lived through demons of my own.

Inner turmoil distorts and denies the power of the words
to hurt or to heal.
And so I wielded the sword until grabbing the wrong end.
Felt the blade cut into my own heart
and the hearts of the people that I claimed I loved.

In the darkest moments of my life
Somewhere between a heartbreaking reality
and a perpetual nightmare,

I heard my Heavenly Father's whisper in the stillness,
Come to me.
You who are heavy laden; I will give you rest.
Sweeter words previously seen yet unknown.

In my most hopeless of moments,
the words blared through my heart
like a huge caste iron bell.
Echoes remain long after the bell in the tower is rung—
getting softer and softer as the last dong trails off
and past shadows are swooped up in the whirling wind.
My hardened heart softened at the invitation.

Urged and enabled by grace, I forgave my husband
As I hoped those that I hurt would forgive me.

Words. Flesh-eating words rendered toothless in the
presence of God. No longer enemies.
But long lost friends that went out of their way to find me.

Take a moment to remember a time when God
interceded for you. Remember a time or situation where
He saved you from yourself.

As painful it may have been—you got through
it—God being your helper.

Remember. Gratitude and hope are jostled and
rises to the top as we recall across the scenes of our minds
and write it down or express it in some other way.

A few simple paragraphs starting with *God I
remember the time that I (your testimony) but You (enter
what God did for you).*

Or draw it, make a collage, pen a rap, poem, or
sing about your experience. It is something between you
and God—an offering of sorts. A purification of the most
intimate kind. Offer it up to the Lord as a sacrifice of
thanksgiving and remembrance that you've been through
the fire and come out on the other side as pure gold. God
is on the Throne of your life—still.

BEYOND THE FIERY FURNACE

"If we are thrown into the blazing furnace, the God we serve is able to save us from it, and he will rescue us from your hand, O king. But even if he does not, we want you to know, O king, that we will not serve your gods or worship the image of gold you have set up." So said, Shadrach, Meshach and Abednego, to the king Nebuchadnezzar.

Daniel Chapter 3 goes on to recount that the king had the furnace fired up 7 times hotter than usual. The fire was so hot the soldiers were incinerated as they approached the door, as Shadrach, Meshach, and Abednego—firmly tied—fell into the fire. Then, the king in amazement asked his advisors, "Weren't there three men that we tied up and threw into the fire?" They replied, "Certainly, O king."

You remember the rest of the story, right? The king exclaimed, "Look! I see four men walking around in the fire, unbound and unharmed, and the fourth looks like a son of the gods."

Yes! I say. And His name is the King of Kings a/k/a Jesus!

They saw that the fire had not harmed their bodies, nor was a hair of their heads singed; their robes were not scorched, and there was no smell of fire on them.

Then Nebuchadnezzar said, "Praise be to the God of Shadrach, Meshach and Abednego, who has sent his angel and rescued his servants! They trusted in him and defied the king's command and were willing to give up their lives rather than serve or worship any god except their own God. Therefore I decree that the people of any nation or language who say anything against the God of Shadrach, Meshach and Abednego be cut into pieces and their houses be turned into piles of rubble, for no other god can save in this way."

And the story could have ended there and it would have been powerful enough. But God took it a step further.

Verse 30 tells us the ending and perhaps the purpose of the story: Then the king promoted Shadrach, Meshach and Abednego in the province of Babylon.

Perhaps you've been going through your season of storms and testing. Sometimes, you feel like you are in the fiery furnace. Like Shadrach, Meshach and Abednego, we are not alone—Jesus shows up on our behalf. Though the fire rages around us, it will not touch us either. We feel God's presence like a cool trade wind on a hot Caribbean day.

Though the flames lick at our feet and mind—we mustn't faint nor complain. We must trust even though sometimes fear grips us—we don't live in the fear because God has not given us a spirit of fear but of power, of love and a sound mind.

There is something else perhaps more profound that I take from this account of Shadrach, Meshach, and Abednego. The fact that God trusted them with the responsibility of experiencing the fiery furnace as well as the subsequent honor wrought from the experience.

It was their faith that now fans the flame of our own faith and countless others—as many as the sands on the universe's shores. Who's to say they were not afraid but they didn't live in their fear. And they thought it better to perish with God then live without Him.

And when we begin to feel that the flames will surely consume us, God brings a person, song, verse, a mesmerizing crimson sunset, a soul-stirring sermon, a smile, or a quiet moment where we feel doused with His peace, which somehow assures us that we are not alone.

Like the Shadrach, Meshach, and Abednego of antiquity, who brought—with their action—glory to God, we, too when tested and purified in the fire, if we hold fast to the promises of God regardless of how dismal it looks or how hopeless we feel, we too, will be brought out of our fiery furnaces *unbound* and *unharmed* and not even smelling like smoke.

Together, we must hold on to see what the end's gonna be.

DEAR HEAVENLY FATHER,

We've made some unhealthy choices in our lifetimes. Who knows that fact better than You? Yet, You've kept your promises to us. You've been faithful even when we are faithless. Bless and have mercy on us. Lift us in Your love and whisper to us of our special-ness to You that no one can take away—ever!

We love You and we're reaching out—seeking Your face. Make it so plain to us that YOU are here; never to leave or forsake us, and that the best is yet to be. Heal our broken hearts and bind up all my wounds. May our relationship with You become stronger and many more testimonies be birthed out of our experiences with You; so that we may bless others as You bless us. Amen. So be it!

CHAPTER 3: FAITH REMEMBERS

"God works all things together for the good
of those who love Him
and are called according to His purposes."
Romans 8:28 (NIV)

THE ONE THAT GOT AWAY

♫*Slippin' into darkness. Pretty soon you'll have to pay.*♫
I'm the one that got away
Didn't deserve to
Didn't have the nerve to stop it.
IT stopped me.
Damn near killed me.
Once, Twice, Three times dead from an overdose
Yet breath came back to me that I didn't willfully breathe

♫*Slippin' into darkness. Pretty soon you'll have to pay.*♫

I'm the one that got away!
Friends, partners, running buddies died all around me
Poor health care, stabbings, boyfriends loving them to
death, gunshot wounds, overdoses, STDs and AIDS.

Evette, Joe, Sister, Ronald, Gloria, a lover but I don't
remember his name.
Now that's insane. All that connected us was the heroin
and emotional pain.

Loneliness, hopelessness, degradation, despair, and
staggering shame
Sucking my soul dry and withering my dreams until my
life was unrecognizable.
A smoldering ember left to fall into the fire.

♫*Slippin' into darkness. Pretty soon you'll have to pay.*♫
But I'm the one that got away.

No way did I deserve it
God just threw a curve ball and I caught it
A hit of faith
shocked the shame right out of me
the constant pain of living with the night and day-mares
terrifying thoughts of foaming at the mouth like a rabid
dog, dying in a glass-strewn alley.
Tossed out of a dope house after an overdose like a
tainted bloody needle.

♫*Slippin' into darkness. Pretty soon you'll have to pay.*♫

In my dying-hour, I heard a whisper,
"The truth will set you free.

But truth is the ESSENCE and not a BY-PRODUCT
strained from lies."

Truth-never-be-told lies, living-lies-walking, 20-year-
sequestered secrets
ruptured and oozed from my mind and soul
like pus from an infected open wound.
Sent me to my knees.

♫*Slippin' into darkness. Pretty soon you'll have to pay.*♫
Thief? Guilty
Abortion? Guilty
Abandoned my son? Guilty
Unforgiving? Guilty
Selfish-by-nature? Guilty
Sorry? YES!
Forgiven? Yes!

♫*Slippin' into darkness. Pretty soon you'll have to pay.*♫

I'm the one that got away.
Such tenderness and grace I'd never known
Even with the tainted seeds I'd sewn,
I can't explain it. Makes no sense to me.
I was dead to EVERYTHING good and now I'm ALIVE
and totally FREE.

I'm the one that got away.

A small voice for ones hushed prematurely
That could have easily been me.
Through the one that got away,
WE LIVE and share the hope another day.

♫Excerpt *Slippin' Into Darkness, as sung by the R&B group, War.*

I REMEMBER WHEN

I remember when I went to my first 12-step meeting at the Trust Clinic in Washington, DC. The first person I saw that I knew was Frankie, my hit doctor.

For months, I looked for Frankie but he was missing-in-action. As my hit-doctor, I normally paid Frankie $5.00 or a portion of my heroin to find a vein in my neck willing to receive the contents of my hypodermic syringe. Nobody could "hit" me like Frankie. He was gifted--and missing no more.

On a side row of chairs with the sunlight streaming through the open blinds, there appeared to be a halo framing Frankie's tall, lean body. He smiled and seemed to take no thought of his missing front teeth as he chatted with the young woman beside him. His legs were crossed as he confidently sported feet clad in opened-stringed, dull-but-shined black combat boots.

"Frankie! Hey Frankie, where you been? I've been looking for you!"

"Hey, girl! I been right here. Coming to these meetings. I'm clean now."

"What? Clean! Frankie, you not shooting dope no more?"

"No, Stacey. I've been clean for 9 months."

"Nine months, Frankie! Nine whole months!!!!"

"Yeah, girl! Glad to see you here, have a seat. You're gonna be alright."

Bewildered, I sought further explanation. "Wait a minute, Frankie, you ain't using nothing? No reefer? No liquor? No beer? Nothing, Frankie?"

"Nothing, Stacey. For real! Welcome to the program. We've been waiting for you."

"We?"

I was interrupted by a heavy-set woman in the chair in the front of the room, "Hello Family, My name is Della and I'm an addict. Welcome to the noon meeting of..."

I glanced back at Frankie. He smiled and in a low voice said, "Just keep coming back, Stacey. It does get better."

I scanned the room filled with of people of various races and ages. I settled into my end chair about 3 rows from the back of the room. As I looked across the room at the serene-version of Frankie, my ex-hit doctor, a peace flooded my soul. I sensed that my steps were indeed ordered by the Lord and that if He could change Frankie's life, surely He could change mine."

So began my journey in the 12-step program. My one day clean has become 25 years and counting—one day at a time.

What God does for one; He will do for another.

BUSTIN' LOOSE

It started out so flam and glam.

A fly girl for real.

Diamonds. Errand boys. Trips.

A hustler's woman—kept in grand style.

Good government job by day, Go-Go and after-hour joints by night.

♫ *I feel like bustin' loose. Bustin' loose. Take it to the bridge y'all.* ♫

      Somewhere it turned on me.

I stepped across an invisible line into a steady spiraling descent that landed me in hospitals, and a jail cell envying the roaches because they can go in and out of the bars and I couldn't.

Locked inside my greatest fear.

That rather than die, I'd exist in obligatory misery.

No, don't weep for me!

So what I'm the middle of a senseless raging sea.

Ain't no thing. I can handle IT before IT handles me.

♫ *I feel like bustin' loose. Bustin' loose. Take it to the bridge y'all.** ♫

*lyrics from Bustin' Loose by Chuck Brown

47

STANICE ANDERSON

CHANGIN'

♫ *I only meant to wet my feet but you pulled me in.*

*Oh the waters of **addiction** run deep.* ♫

Deeper than my secrets growing rampant in the dark.

Do you hear them? Grumbling like hunger pangs just below the surface like cancer cells growing.

Poised to kill slowly, methodically, insidiously.
Eating away at my conscience,
Turning into life-altering shots of heroin and cocaine.
Jetting out of hypodermic syringe needles plunged into the nucleus of my soul.

The weed, pills, liquor, beer, blotter acid, men, shopping, working, sexual encounters-of-the-not-so-subtle-kind, loosing jobs, STDs, abscesses, desperation, joblessness, homelessness

CHANG-ING seats on the Titanic
CHANG-ING seats on the Titanic
CHA-CHA-CHANG-ING seats on the Titanic

But the ship's STILL going down.
It's a good day to die.

IN MY FATHER'S HOUSE

I never met her. She died before I was born. But if I sit still and listen in the silence, I can see and hear her in my mind. My great-grandmother, a dark heavy woman with a wide sharp nose, sits on the splintering wood step of a paint chipped porch. On a sticky hot summer day, fanning flies with a square of cardboard stapled to a tongue presser that reminded all within view that Mason's Funeral Home was a party-line call away.

The shade tree overhanging the porch provides the only respite from the fierce August-in-the-Nations-Capital noonday sun. The smell of a scratch-cake baking.

"Don't you go in that house, Stanley! I don't want my cake falling," she might have said. "You're not that thirsty you can't wait. Work up some spit and swallow that 'cause you ain't going in that house and that's all there is to it."

In my mind, I can see and hear the tall, lanky 10-year-old boy who was destined to become my father kicking the dirt as he sits down on a patch of grass and mumbles under his breath what he dares not say out loud.

Every Saturday afternoon after the housework was done, children in the neighborhood gathered around my great-grandmother's feet as she told the most wonderful stories. My father told me that her dramatic storytelling mesmerized and transported them to places that only the imagination could take colored children in the restrictive days of Jim Crow.

49

Her voice is like an artist's brush, the honeysuckled air is her canvas, and the words are the pictures that she paints. She strokes the stories into existence and makes the children feel like anything is possible and that whatever their fertile young minds can imagine is highly probable—if they believe!

She is a weaver of words and a planter of hope and dreams—a storyteller.

Perhaps it was there at her feet that my father was bequeathed a legacy of words. Or perhaps the words flowed through her blood and were passed down in a pulsation of parental passion to my father to pass on to future generations.

Thus, the legacy of words and rhythms continue to flow freely through our family's veins and hearts. They bring us comfort and healing, joy and understanding, tears and laughter, pain and pleasure, and above all, hope and promise. The words are gifts that come from my Father's house chosen and wrapped by the mighty Hand of God.

We open the gifts and offer the world generational tastes of words and rhythms, spread before you like multi-colored blankets onto thick carpets of grass.

Come. Let's sit on the splintering wood step under the cool shadow of my great-grandmother's shade tree. Pour yourself a glass of ice-cold water if you'd like. No need to walk softly now, the scratch-cake is done.

We are weavers of words and planters of hope and dreams—storytellers.

MARVIN'S MUSIC
(Written by my Son, Mike E. Tucker, Jr.)

Mom pranced around the room with Marvin
Pipe in one hand, lighter in the other

      "Dance with me, come on dance with me.
Baby in her womb
Flyin' high in the friendly skies
over dust clouds, dope streams and stuff she'd snuff
without ever touching the ground

How that sound?
once reel to reel
now compact disk on repeat
no wonder I can't sleep
see my dreams through residued retinas
never saw me using clearly viewed selling and abusing-

      mothers like mine-
walk no further than the corner
watched her roll cigarettes, take pills she called aspirin
never asking about the bottle caps and incense,

      I just let it play
A hook that is my addiction
I want you. You want me?
how much you got?

      Dance with me.

ODE TO STANICE

(Written by my Father, Stanley J. Anderson, Sr.)

Yes, she was our first-born.
For a name, I was torn.
We reviewed the Anderson Family Tree,
And yes, I was very proud you see.
So we narrowed it down to just two,
Alice, Lucretia, Mary, and ME.

Then we chose STANICE as key.
Never thinking of maybe Stacey,

But off to school she went,
Her playmates and friends did decide,
And they all loved STANICE the Best,
We all that know her, hear the rest.

In school she was intelligent and quick,
Didn't take long to make English and Math mix.
Her favorite teachers were Mrs. Dennis, Gwen Johnson
and then!

Her interest turned to boys and young men.
She was attractive and well built,
Well, male instincts were very true
As she attended Birney, Douglas, and Ballou.

Cutting school became her Rule,
And Reading, Writing, Poetry
became an Interest and Tool.

She later gave birth to a son named Mike.
A rugged and likeable little "Tike."
So, from Morgan University he will graduate in June,

52

Aided by hard work and a "Mind" well focused and
tuned.

Of MIKE and STANICE, I'm proud they are also Mine!

Praise the LORD, we all do say—
They are making IT, in a Beautiful Way.
Now, Tomorrow and forever more,
They are two Beautiful People
"Down to the CORE"!!!

©1998 Stanley James Anderson, Sr. (September 24, 1927 -
November 4, 1998)

    In 2010, while surfing the internet, I happened
across a District of Columbia City Council official
document* dated May 17, 2005. To my amazement, it
named a city street in Anacostia area of Washington,
D.C., "Anderson Place, S.E.," in honor of my dad. To my
knowledge, no one in my family was notified.

    I got directions online. My son drove my mother
and I to Anderson Place, minutes from our family home
on Stanton Road, where my brother and I were raised. We
took turns taking photos of each other under *our* street
sign as we talked, laughed and got teary-eyed exchanging
memories. My dad loved Washington, DC, Anacostia
community and its' people. He worked hard to affect
positive change. It made me smile to think it loved him
back. More than a weaver of words and planter of hope
and dreams—a respected leader and my Daddy.

  *Committee of the Whole Report Re: Bill 16-196 "…Anderson
Place, S.E., is named for Stanley J. Anderson, a resident east of the
Anacostia River, who held several positions in the District
government and served on the appointed D.C. Council."

I WANT TO WRITE A POEM FOR YOU
(Written by Daughter of Stan; Mother of Mike)

I want to write a poem for you
A rhyme for you
Rhythms and nuances
Not so subtle highs and lows
Peaks and valleys
Summits and twenty thousand leagues
beyond
All I could see
Where next generations
Rise to the top

I want to write a poem for you
A rhyme for you
In three-quarter time for you
One-of-a-kind for you
From breast to brain
From the heart to a train
Of thought
That leaves you breathless
To think it
My cup runneth over with legacy
So drink deep
Words for the weaving
Stories for the telling

A rhyme for you
In three-quarter time for you
I wrote this poem for you.

In spite of all we did and obstinently refused to do, God did not remove or withhold His gifts from us. We may not hone or use them but they exist. Perhaps they are hidden under the *dust and cobwebs* of our unexplored potential. Our gifts and talents are waiting to be discovered and shared with a world so desperately in need of the gifts we were born to bring to this table of life.

From generation to generation, let's go to God and ask Him to ignite all that He designed us to be so that we can be about our Father's business.

TASTE AND SEE!

I sat on the red-cushioned pew beside my mentor, Dorine. With a slow, barely noticeable sway, her eyes closed and not bothering to look at the hymnal she sang the chorus,

♫ *He's sweet I know. Dark clouds may rise, and strong winds may blow. But, I tell the world, wherever I may go. That I have found a Savior and He's sweet I know.* * ♫

I sensed her relationship with God in the calmly offered love billowing heavenward on the wings of the melody. It was like she sang only to Him; not caring if she was on key, or if she missed a few words. No matter. So personal. So intimate. So real.

Silently, I prayed, "God, I'd like to know you and be known by you like that."

I met Dorine during a time during my life where I desperately needed a mentor; someone willing to show me how to live a drug-free life and how to forgive myself for the wrong choices I made.

In those moments, it was clear that it was not a coincidence that we met. It was as if God engineered our paths crossing. And now, years later, sitting in the pew next to her with my heart stirred up and on fire for Jesus. how sweet!

I tasted God's love. Oh yes! In the ordinariness of the days and in subtle beautiful moments like these, I tasted His love. In His love letter, the Bible, He reminded me in every phrase, chapter and verse, and in every story; Yes, I'm reminded how high, wide and deep God's unconditional love is. So sweet, I know.

Have I tasted? Hummmm. I let the song's melody meld with the gratitude of my heart lead me into God's Throne Room. I sensed my nearness to God and allowed it to take me out of the pew and into long forgotten scenes from my life like on pages of a play.

Page turned. There, the day I died three times in the ambulance on the way to the hospital after a heroin overdose. God had the last word after each flat line— Breathe! Obediently, oxygen rushed into my lifeless body—so sweet.

From memory to memory, my thoughts danced to the rhythm of God's Grace.

Page turned. The dark night in my life, alone and shooting heroin in my apartment, I saw an addict's testimony reenacted on a television show, *The 700 Club*, and I was so moved that I prayed and asked Jesus to do for me what He had evidently done in that man's life. I prayed, "Set me free from the bondage of my addiction, forgive me, give me a new life, and change my eternal destiny." He did it! God did it that night. My apartment flooded with brilliant light that chased hopelessness from my life.

Page turned. I remembered the day I called a family friend, Reverend John Kinard, who immediately went into action and arranged my admission into an inpatient addiction treatment program. God's answer to prayers delivered me from heroin addiction and deposited me into a brand new life in Jesus. Surrounded by caring family, friends, 12-step programs, churches, and *The 700 Club*, caring people helped me rebuild my life, resurrect my dreams, ignite my desire to discover and passionately live God's plans and purposes for me—so sweet!

Page turned. For months the doctor couldn't stop my menstrual cycle. He wanted to operate; but I had a new job and had to wait until my health insurance kicked in.

Through it all, God kept me. I was weak, yes. I had a few embarrassing moments in public places, yes. But I kept my pace and my family and friends, didn't let me give in to discouragement or despair.

Through it all, I learned to trust God and not be afraid.

Cleared by my insurance company for surgery, the orderlies rolled me on the gurney into the Operating Room. As the anesthesiologist prepared me for surgery, my right ovary burst. According to my doctor, had I been anywhere other than the operating table, I would have died.

Page turned. I tasted God as He removed my desire for cigarettes after having smoked since I was 15 years old. On the third day after quitting, I wanted a cigarette so bad—relapse seemed imminent. I prayed, *"Lord, do for me what I can't do for myself right now— hold on and not smoke.* Minutes later the phone rang. It was my son, "Moms, I heard you quit smoking. Is it true?"

"Yep, this is day three of not smoking a cigarette—one day at a time. But right now it feels like I have to take it one minute at a time."

He wanted to come by the house to see me; so I said, "fine."

When he got there, he hugged me and confessed something profound. I'll never forget it. As we sat on the couch with his head resting on my shoulder he said, "Do you realize that in my 25 years of living, I have never NOT smelled you smelling like cigarettes?"

I cried and asked him to forgive me and wondered how I could have been so oblivious to his desire, need, and right to have a smoke-free mommy. I thought of the 25 years of second-hand smoke. How selfish. How wrong! That phone call, knock on the door, and bitter truth, gave me what I needed to well up the determination that it takes to remain nicotine free. A bitter pill swallowed; but miraculously only sweetness remained.

Page turned. When my doctor nonchalantly announced during my routine visit, "You know you have Hepatitis C right?"

Shocked, I responded, "No!"

She continued, "Yes, the blood test reveals that you do."

Relaxed but assertive, I instructed, "Then, please order another blood test. I've been clean for 22 years and have had more than enough blood tests. And never have I been told that I had Hep C." She wrote out the order for another blood test.

On my way home, I prayed and poured out my heart to God. Afterwards, I sealed it all with a phone call to my best friend, Omie, and shared my latest burden. Then, I determined in my heart to let go and let God work it out for me. I proceeded with the next item on my life's to-do list.

A week later, I went back to the clinic and found that my doctor was no longer on staff and had been replaced. The new doctor took me to his office, my file already opened on his desk, he said, "Your blood work shows that you do not have Hepatitis C; however, it indicates that you were exposed to Hepatitis C at some point in your past and that your body fought it off."

Right there sitting beside his computer I let out a rather loud uncontainable, "Thank you, Jesus!" I knew the One who fought it off for me. Without a doubt in my mind, King Jesus fights all my battles! How sweet!

Two months later, my mammogram showed two masses in my left breast. I prayed about it, talked to my friends, and went on with my life list again.

The surgeon informed me that if I waited a couple of weeks, the hospital would have a new sonar machine that would allow him to get a biopsy and remove the masses at the same time with a laser probe through a tiny incision. I waited for the machine and went on with my life list.

When surgery day came, with a local anesthesia, I watched the doctor on the sonar screen as he maneuvered the laser probe and extracted what he could of the masses. He couldn't get it all but the biopsy of the tissue he retrieved revealed the remaining masses were benign. No cancer! "But let's take another look six months," my doctor suggested.

Page turned. Fast forward. The follow-up breast mammogram and sonogram, reveled the inexplicable—no signs of masses—anywhere. Poof. Gone. I am because God is sweet, I know.

Your page turned. Take a few minutes to remember, reflect, savor, and thank Him for the specifics in your life. In other words, testify to yourself and then to somebody else about the goodness of the Lord in the land of the living. "Have you tasted and seen God's love?" Then, tell somebody…

♫ *He's sweet I know. Dark clouds may rise, and strong winds may blow. But, I tell the world, wherever I may go. That I have found a Savior and He's sweet I know.* ♫

Author/Publisher unknown, *He's Sweet I Know*, public domain

REMEMBERING HAPPY

♫ *It came upon a midnight clear, that glorious song of old.* ♫ Well, no it was more like 6:00 pm, in 11-year old time.

In the kitchen, my momma baked her signature coconut layer cakes. The sweet, touch-of-vanilla smell wafts upstairs. My stomach rumbles in anticipation. The whining buffer machine whizzed as my dad neared the end of his annual Christmas strip-sand-wax our hardwood floors project that—I think was more for the many holiday visitors—than those of us who lived there. The smell and crackle of the logs burning and transitioning themselves in the dining room fireplace's hearth found its way upstairs.

In my bedroom, I looked out at the newly fallen snow glistening under the street lamps. I savored the smells and sounds that bombarded my senses and proved, beyond a shadow of a doubt, that Christmas was amazingly and wonderfully near. With my index finger, I wrote "M-e-r-r-y" across the hazed condensation on my cold window pane.

My 4-year-old brother, burst into my room like an unwanted cherry pit. He grabbed my hand and pulled me toward the door. "Come on, Neicy, come on! It's time."

"Wait!" I abruptly stopped and like a stretched rubber band, his little body slung back into my side. I opened the green frilled window curtains and peered out. Satisfied, I turned and looked down at brother. "Okay, let's go".

Two kids on a mission, we clopped down the stairs, jumped over the whirling buffer being skillfully maneuvered by our Dad who had a mission of his own.

My brother held his arms up and I hoisted him so he could reach the light switch panel. He gleefully flipped up the first two switches. We peeped out the front door window at the amazing Christmas light show.

The tall cedar tree's new coat of snow glistened under the blue, yellow, and red lights. Rudolph's brightly lit red nose led the way as our jolly white Santa's twinkly sleigh appeared suspended in the air and headed to our roof. With a gigantic smile, my brother squealed out his "Ooohs and Ahhhs!"

"Good job!" I assured him and gently placed his feet on the freshly shined hardwood floor.

Mission accomplished, my brother got off to a running start and slid his way into living room. "I did it. I did it by myself," he announced to mom and dad.

Now, for my mission, I thought as I climbed the stairs and headed back to my bedroom. The buffer stopped again and my dad offered his strong suggestion, "Not too loud, now."

"Okay, Daddy." Once in my bedroom, I reached into my closet and put on my hooded coat. Then, I gently lifted the gray box encased record player. I put it on the edge of my dresser, opened the window, and as the cold December air stole into my bedroom, I pulled on my hood.

Leaning outside my window, I cleared a patch of snow from the aluminum awning over the side porch for the speaker and closed the window gently on the cord that led to the turntable on my dresser.

I turned on the power, lifted the record player's arm and rested it on the first of the evening's Christmas picks. Turning the volume to a respectful 7 out of 10, I released our gift of music into the neighborhood. Johnny Mathis' smooth as melted chocolate voice enveloped the frost bitten night, ♫ *Hark the Harold angels sing, glory to the newborn king.* ♫

"Neicy! Make sure you close the window. We're not heating the neighborhood. Come downstairs when you're done. I made us some hot cocoa."

"Okay, Momma." With my finger, I scribbled the letters C-h-r-i-s-t-m-a-s through the cold and wet condensation on the window below the fading M-e-r-r-y, and shouted, "I'm coming."

Mission accomplished; I shed my coat, turned toward my bedroom door, and followed my mother's voice. I felt extremely happy, as I sang my way downstairs.

♫ *Chestnuts roasting on an open fire, Jack Frost nipping at your nose. Although it's been said many times many ways, Merry Christmas to you.* ♫

Perhaps there's a day that you remember as a happy time. A day filled with love as soothing as a warm cup of cocoa on a frigid winter's evening. Remember a happy time when infinite possibilities laid before you like virgin paths of newly fallen snow. A joyous time when thoughts of sugar plums danced in your head and reindeer could fly.

Remembering these times helps us strengthen our faith and press our way through the ordinary and difficult days.

The Bible encourages us "whatever is true, whatever is noble, whatever is right, whatever is pure, whatever is lovely, whatever is admirable—if anything is excellent or praiseworthy—think about such things." (Philippians 4:8 NIV).

I AM THAT I AM is The God of Then, Now and Forevermore. Ask Him to help you remember *happy*. He will.

The Christmas Song ©1944, Mel Tormé and Bob Wells

CHICKEN LITTLE, THE SKY IS GRIEVING

The Sky is Grieving
It seems the sky is in grief mode.
Sobbing bitterly on and off all day and night and day—
and night.
It tries to get it together—
perhaps wanting to impress the Sun

> *I can handle this. I can handle this.*

And then it's like it remembers the pain again and BAM
Thunder, lightning and uncontrollable sobbing—
feeling the pain of the world.

Chicken Little, the Sky is Grieving
The Sky is Grieving for us.

A NEW BEGINNING

On some untraceable day, I crossed the imaginary line from recreational drug use to full-blown heroin addiction. Rejected by most of my family and friends, I lived alone and on the brink of eviction in an efficiency apartment. I cried often, and in-between sobs and self-pity, I stole, lied, schemed, and sold my body to supply my drug habit. I had an acquired soul sickness disease that my self-prescribed regimen of drugs no longer masked.

By the time I was 35, every corner and crevice of my life hurt and I was convinced that it was too late to change. I existed in a constant state of hopelessness and despair. My spirit was dead and my body was tired of the vicious cycle and downward spiral of addiction—living to use and using to live.

I imagined myself dying on a bitterly cold night sprawled in a debris-strewn alley under a flickering street lamp as I foamed at the mouth like a rabid dog. I decided that a death as hard as my wretched life would be poetic justice.

Instead, alone in my bathroom one February evening, I stood in front of the mirror and injected a heroin/cocaine mixture into my hand and neck. Then, I walked through the living room toward the kitchen to get some Kool-Aid™.

Before I got there, I heard a man's southern drawled voice coming from my 13-inch black and white television. He talked of his heroin addiction and the consequences.

However, he also talked of grace.

Drawn to his words, I sat on my mattress on the floor in front of the TV. Buddy Baird was the name that flashed under his image. I wondered how The 700 Club was on the TV. I never looked at that show for fear that it might provide God with a window into my life.

Although Buddy spoke of hopelessness, his elegantly chiseled white face with half-parted lips turning into a smile every time he said, "But Jesus . . ." gleamed like a diamond under a noonday sun. He explained that he found a way out. Rather, a way out found him.

I could not take my eyes off his handsome face. I yearned for the kind of peace and joy that resided in his eyes. Tired and disgusted with myself, it seemed like my soul shouted out, *Talk to me, And Buddy. Tell me. What did you do? If you were where I am, how did you get out?* I queried Buddy as if he was in the room with me. I watched intently and waited for his answers.

In an instant, the station switched from a live interview to a video re-enactment of his story that was too much like mine. In one scene, Buddy stood by a window with a mirror and a heroin-filled syringe up to his neck as He searched for a willing vein. All of a sudden, it was not him I saw on the television screen, but it was me.

For the first time, I saw the unadulterated truth about what I had become—a desolate and addicted woman who desperately wanted to live but did not know how. Like a carefully aimed laser in the skilled hands of a surgeon, Buddy Baird's story penetrated and disintegrated my thick wall of denial. Like a warm melted healing salve the message that he carried of Jesus' love, forgiveness and power dripped into my aching soul.

However, there were rumors in my head that had been there so long that I believed them. Rumors like "you can't teach old dog new tricks" and because of the way I lived, I felt like an old dog. Another one that weighed me down as if a cord of logs tied around my neck was "You have to get your life right first and then go to God." As if Buddy heard my thoughts he answered, "But Jesus came into my life and took my desire for drugs away. He changed me."

I wept as his words awakened my soul from a deep sleep and stirred my thoughts in a new direction, *"Since Jesus changed Buddy's life, perhaps He will do the same for me."* With a child's heart, I seized the moment. Since I was already on the floor, I turned over onto my knees and prayed, "Jesus, help me. Do for me what you did for Buddy. Forgive me for my sins. I believe that You died for me and rose again. Come into my heart and live Your life in me. Be my Lord and Savior. Amen."

Immediately, a strong sense of forgiveness and peace inflated my withered spirit like a hand slipped into soft silk glove. I felt the burdens and sins of a lifetime whooshed away in a moment of sublime grace. A brilliant light flooded my apartment and I got up as if to welcome God into my life.

Without thought, long-held secrets poured out of my heart and up through my lips. I uttered harm done to me and harm done by me. I confessed jealousies and resentments that were festering ulcers parasitically attached to my soul. Without trepidation, things that I dared not whisper in the dark, I exposed to God's light.

In the next moment, it was as if I heard the Lord say, *"I know. I saw you in the pigsty. I kept you alive through it all. I forgive you. You are preciously mine and I love you."*

That frigid night in February turned out to be the warmest night of my life. I crossed over from hopelessness to hope and from death to life.

Soon after, a pastor arranged my admission into an addiction treatment facility. I have enjoyed an intimate personal relationship with God through Jesus Christ and freedom from heroin addiction for more than twenty years. To think that the God of the universe came and walked with me, talked with me and told me I was His own—it's all too marvelous!

THE GIFT

It was December 1984. I was in treatment on the first floor of the drug treatment center on the grounds of St. Elizabeth Hospital in Southeast, Washington, D.C. Although only a few weeks clean, I counted down the hours to attend the 12-step program meetings that were brought into the center. My peers called me *strange* and other names that I care not to recall or recant. It hurt not to be considered a part of yet another group of my peers. But such was life for me. I had to deal with the feelings. This time, however, without alcohol or narcotics.

Could anyone not see that I needed to know that someone cared for me—whether I stayed clean or not or that I was still breathing? Would love forever elude me? These were the questions that invaded my mind—confirming my aloneness.

And then, the muffled sound of the people grew loud and clear. It was the clapping that brought me back to the moments at hand. Someone from the outside won the raffle. Going to redeem her prize was a beautiful black woman, neatly dressed, head held high, eyes bright and telling.

Telling me softly as she took a moment to look my way, "Better days are yet to be. Hold on, my sister."

As the secretary of the meeting embraced her in a sisterly hug, she gave her the "Big Book," as they called it. The winner turned and proceeded back to her seat.

Looking down at the floor, with a prayer in my heart, I wondered how long before my better day. My whole life hurt and there were so many things wrong—including being 34 years old and in an addiction treatment center.

I felt a gentle touch on my arm. I looked up from where I sat. It was the winner. She smiled down at me and pressed the big blue and white covered book into my hands. "For you," she said.

"For me?"

"Yes. Here", she said, as she reached for the book. "Let me write something in it. What is your name?" she asked as she kneeled down beside me with pen in hand.

"Stanice."

"Now, you have to spell that one for me."

I did. She smiled, as she wrote on the inside front cover of the book, handed it back to me and regally walked to her seat.

The second half of the meeting began for everyone but me. I was in my own world.

I opened the front cover and read, "Stanice, please keep coming back. Love, Evelyn."

My tears refused to be held back to a more private time. I turned in my seat to see if I could locate my benefactor. There she was. Our eyes met. Tasting the saltiness of my tears, I silently mouthed, "Thank you so much."

She nodded as if to say, "it's okay and you're going to be okay."

I turned back around in my seat but it was also a turning point in my life. God answered my unspoken prayer. I knew that at least one person cared about me. A woman named Evelyn.

Her gift keeps on giving—25 years later, I am still alcohol and drug-free!

THE LETTER

After my friend and I got over the initial excitement of talking to one another for the first time in over 14 years, Raymond said, "Stanice, you probably don't remember that letter that you wrote to me."

I didn't.

But he continued, "Whenever I was discouraged, I pulled the letter out and read it. Your words energized and reminded me that I had a friend, God only knew where, who cared about me, believed in me, and wanted only good things for me. I hoped that one day God would allow our paths to cross again and I could tell you how much that letter has meant to me over the years."

My eyes filled with tears as I felt God's love wrap me in my friend's soft words. I said, "I sure would like to see what I wrote all those years ago?"

"I'll show you the letter when I come to see you."

Astonished I said, "You've got to be kidding! You still have it?"

"I sure do. It's still in great condition." He continued, "Your words are as fresh today as the day you penned them almost 20 years ago."

Today, which is all we have so far, write a letter to encourage someone. Yes, write a letter to a new friend, an old friend, a family member—whomever, wherever, as the Lord leads.

Pray. Ask God who He wants you to write. In the stillness of a moment within your day, I believe that person's name will be laid upon your mind like a soft down pillow. You will know exactly who you are to write an old fashioned hand-written, stamped and mailed not e-mailed letter. It doesn't have to be long—keep it as simple as you can.

Allow the words to pour from your heart and splash onto the page. Before mailing the letter, pray for the person as the Holy Spirit leads. Let it go and watch God produce fruit that will last.

DEAR HEAVENLY FATHER:

I thank You that you know all things, see all things, and are in everything good. I also thank You that there is nothing that I don't go through that is not already sifted through Your fingers. So I come to You, with a child's heart and in all humility asking You to work out the situation that confronts me. Give me the strength, the wisdom and discernment to know what to say, how to say it, when to say it and with the right heart to say it.

Let it fall on ears and a heart that You've tilled first and made ready to receive in the love that it is intended. I will follow Your lead and then leave the outcome to You. You work it all out together for the good of those who love You and who You have called according to Your purposes. I thank You that You alone are God and are all I need. I bless Your Name and count it all done as I lay this and all burdens down at the foot of the cross and now—rest in YOU. In Jesus' Name, I ask this and all things. Amen. So be it!

CHAPTER 4: FAITH LAUGHS

"Do not grieve, for the joy of the LORD is your strength."
Nehemiah 8:10 (NIV)

STANICE ANDERSON

FAITH EXPOSED

What must Faith look like?

A wispy, beautiful celestial being with

Milk and honey tears.

Butterfly wings

Cotton candy hair

A pink rose petal dress

With a waterfall train?

Exquisite jeweled slippers

and diamond footprints

Or a burly, sweaty, unshaven man

In a welder's mask

with a blazing blow torch at the ready?

GOD'S IN THE DETAILS

When I got up out of bed early one April morning, the only thing on my agenda was to do a few chores around the apartment and then bake some of my famous chocolate chip walnut cookies. I wasn't looking to learn any life-changing lessons.

In between the mopping and sweeping, nature called and I listened. As I lifted the toilet lid, I saw a little gray fur ball on the floor—right in front of the toilet. Something was strange about the fur ball. It appeared to be heaving.

Upon closer examination, I saw that this fur ball was actually a mouse! A mouse that was brave enough to lay still right in front of my feet ... at the toilet. Not good.

I really had to go to the bathroom; but I confess that I was afraid of the little furry creature that was not afraid of me. Just in case it was asleep or nodded out from too much baby mouse milk or something, I stamped my foot in an attempt to rouse it. It did not scamper away like I planned. With my eyes locked in on the mouse, I walked backwards out of the bathroom. At this point, I started to shuffle because the call of nature went from a gentle whisper to an urgent cry.

However, the mouse, that apparently was dying, presented a real dilemma for me; especially, since I lived alone in an apartment with only one bathroom. Too embarrassed to knock on my neighbor's door to ask to use theirs, I danced in place while I pondered the predicament that grew dire with each second that passed.

I could go to the kitchen and get an old mayonnaise jar or coffee can. I could have an accident on the floor. Although, I don't think under these circumstances it would be considered an accident. Or the obvious last resort, be a grown woman and sweep up the mouse and toss it out in the backyard.

To prepare myself for the mature option, I paced the floor and recited repeatedly my personalized version of II Timothy 1:7 that I use to combat fear: "God did not give me a spirit of fear but a spirit of power, love and a sound mind."

After several minutes of this exercise, I felt fortified enough to do the deed. Armed with a broom and a dustpan, I bravely marched toward the bathroom and the enemy. I bent down slightly to check his breathing pattern. It did not appear to be heaving. Dead or alive—it didn't matter—the mouse was about to be history.

I positioned the broom and readied myself to stoop for the big scoop. I prayed a quick prayer, "Please, Lord, give me whatever it is I need to get through this."

All of a sudden I thought of an option that I had not thought of before. I stood straight up, turned, walked out of the bathroom, and headed for the back door.

As if to remind me that my priorities were out of kilter, nature shouted its demand, "Go to the bathroom NOW!" Instead, I practically danced to the back door.

I turned the lock, slid back the bolt, opened the back door, and clanked open the steel black barred security door that freed me onto the porch.

It was then that I heard my downstairs neighbor's cat, Patches, "Meow." Before I could invite Patches in, she jumped inside with the stealth of a lioness after its prey. She bolted straight through the apartment, slid on the polished wood slat floor, and made a sharp left into the bathroom.

I ran behind Patches shouting, "Thank you, Jesus! Thank you Jesus!"

Before I could get close to the bathroom, Patches passed me in the left lane with the mouse tucked neatly in her teeth on her way out the back door. Her mission was complete and now I was about to complete mine. I headed straight for the bathroom.

Before that day, I used to wonder, with all that God has to do, could He possibly care about the little details of my life? Patches answered my question that day with a resounding, "Meow!" I believe that was cat talk for "He's an on-time God. Yes He is!"

We need to stop putting God in a box and come to believe that He can act on our behalf, anytime, anywhere, and by any means.

M&M's® MELT IN HIS HAND

"What is it that that the Lord would have me to do, Pastor Finney? What exactly is my calling? Would you ask the Lord for me? I'm aware of some of my gifts, but how do they work together so that He can get even more glory out of my life?"

This was my request to my 101-year-old Pastor of Christ Spiritual Temple Baptist Church. She had been preaching since the Lord healed her from her sick bed at age 32. Who better to ask to confirm my calling than someone so close to and so much in love with Jesus Christ?

"I'll do that for you," she softly assured me and continued, "He'll tell me. I know he will."

Two weeks later, I called her back. "Has the Lord told you yet, Pastor?"

"No, honey, not yet. But, I asked Him. He's gonna do it. He's gonna tells us. In the meantime, you just believe, watch, and pray."

Another week passed. Feeling a strong urge to call Pastor again, I prayed, "I don't want to be a bother, Lord. Is this you prompting me to call her or is it my impatience?"

Wrapped in expectancy and excitement, I dialed the pastor's telephone number. "Hi. It's Stanice. Remember what I asked you to ask the Lord?"

"Sure I do. And He answered!"

I opened my heart, mind, and spirit to receive God's living Word for me. "Who am I in Him, Pastor?"

"The Lord has set you aside for a double anointed ministry. M and M." She paused, left the earthly conversation with me, and praised God, "Thank you, Jesus. Thank you, sweet Jesus..."

Not wanting to interrupt but feeling compelled, I had to ask, "What is "M and M," Pastor Finney?

Excitement was the backdrop of her high-trilled voice. "The Lord showed me that you are a Minister and a Missionary. Yes, He has given you a two-fold ministry!"

Not daring to voice my doubts, I doubted nonetheless. In my heart.

I thought, A minister? That's a confirmation of what you've already shown me. I've been ministering in Your Name for many years. But Missionary? I don't even have a passport.

Lord, shouldn't a missionary at least have a passport?

In an instant, at my heart's core, the Holy Spirit reminded me of the story in the Bible where Sarah overhears God talking with her husband, Abraham.

Then the LORD said, "I will surely return to you about this time next year, and Sarah your wife will have a son." Now Sarah was listening at the entrance to the tent, which was behind him. Abraham and Sarah were already old and well advanced in years, and Sarah was past the age of childbearing. So Sarah laughed to herself as she thought, "After I am worn out and my master is old, will I now have this pleasure?"

Then the LORD said to Abraham, "Why did Sarah laugh and say, 'Will I really have a child, now that I am old?' Is anything too hard for the LORD? I will return to you at the appointed time next year and Sarah will have a son."

Sarah was afraid, so she lied and said, "I did not laugh."

But he said, "Yes, you did laugh." (Genesis 18:10-15 NIV)

I confessed my doubt and felt it die in the light of exposure. "Pastor, I don't understand why the Lord blesses me so." I continued, "But I receive that Word in the Name of Jesus. Let it be according to His will."

Pastor Finney ministered to me a bit longer, and gave me Bible scriptures that God would use to seal His Word to me.

After the call, I knelt before the Lord and prayed, "Father God, please forgive my doubt. As You say, I am Your Minister and Missionary. Send me."

A few weeks later I received this e-mail,

My name is Ann-Marie. My cousin bought me your book...which I believe was God's divine intervention...Your book brought home to me that, with

FAITH and TRUST in God, one can move mountains. Presently, I am involved in a project with my former High School Principal, now my best friend, Sister Pat, in a quest to build a home for young girls in St. Vincent, the Caribbean Island, where I am from originally.

These girls presently are going through some of the experiences that you spoke about yourself in your book.

Every chapter that I read in your book I kept saying "My God! If these Girls at home can get a chance to read this book and meet this woman in person who have overcome so much and has triumphed over it all with Jesus by her side, every step of the way, they might get the FAITH to leap forward with Jesus".

My prayer is that I would like you to come to St. Vincent and speak to these girls...Sister Pat and I are praying that you would journey to the Caribbean to be a voice to the hurting girls.

"Thank you, Jesus!" My words trailed upwards, through my open sunroof, to the powder-puff white clouds of a perfect spring day and stretched all the way to Heaven as I drove to the US Post Office to apply for my first passport.

A few months later, with all expenses paid and accompanied by Ann-Marie, I stood atop the plane's metal stairs, squinting into the seemingly up-close Caribbean sun. The smell of the salty sea tickled my nostrils.

Slowly, I descended the stairs and set foot on the stunning island of St. Vincent.

The Lord used the seven-day trip for tremendous ministry coordinated by Sister Pat Douglass. It included Youth, Women, and Men Gatherings, talks at Catholic and Pentecostal churches, middle and high schools, as well as newspaper, radio and television interviews.

God also provided the blessed Cummings family who allowed me to stay in the guest wing of their hillside home, complete with a private veranda overlooking the kite's string of islands that make up St. Vincent and the Grenadines.

Perhaps as a reward for those who persevered, by mid-week Sister Pat, Ann-Marie, Joyita (one of the girls from the Catholic school), and I took an afternoon for a little R&R. We went swimming in the Caribbean Sea and the salt-water pool at a friend's resort on the private Young Island.

The next time you want to laugh about what God declares over your life? Remember Sarah. Remember me.

THE PINK HOUSE

When I picked up the keys to the new house I was renting from a friend, she confided, "I'm gonna tell you now, Stanice. The walls are pink, but I can have it painted for you later."

Pink? OK, how pink can they be?

Memories of a happy childhood flooded my mind as I walked up onto the porch of the red-brick rowhouse in the Anacostia community where I grew up. I opened the door and stepped up into the vestibule.

Bam! There they were. The walls seemed to scream, "We're hot flamingo pink!" I turned to the left into living room. Eye-squinting pink. Then, through to the archway into the dining room. Miami Beach pink. I made a sharp right into the kitchen. Relief! A cool eggshell white with one blood-red wall. Encouraged, I opted to forgo the basement and headed upstairs. The stairwell? Neon pink! Straight ahead at the top of the stairs, the bathroom was a warm beige. Onward to the guest bedroom. Have you guessed? Hot Flamingo, eye-squinting, Miami Beach, neon PINK!

I made my way slowly down the neon pink hallway. *Will there be another reprieve of color like the kitchen and the bathroom?* I slowly opened the master bedroom door. SURPRISE! Turquoise blue-green walls as rich in color as the Caribbean Sea.

Needing a place to call home and grateful for my friend's generous offer, I signed the lease and moved

87

in. Every day I considered the palettes of calming colors possible for my new place.

A week or so after I moved in, my son brought my grandkids. The elder of the three, Michal Zoe, then four years old, came inside first.

In the wonderment and excitability of a child, she called to her twin brother and sister, "Arin and Nya. Come see! It's pink! Daddy, Hallelujah, Grandma's house is pink!"

Michal Zoe rushed from room to room in glee and amazement, "It's pink!" She ran upstairs and called out as if in one long sentence, "It's all pink. My room is pink, too. Oh, Grandma. It's my favorite color. It's pink! Your room is blue, but you can paint it pink, too."

I interjected, attempting to soften the blow as I announced my plans, "But Michal Zoe, I don't think Grandma can take this much pink. I'm going to have it painted."

"Oh, no, Grandma. You can't. You can't paint it."

"I know it's your favorite color, but ... ."

Michal Zoe looked up at me with those large almond-shaped brown eyes. I knew I would melt under such pressure, but I resolved to stand firm.

Michal Zoe had a resolve of her own, as she calmed herself and gently chided, "But Grandma you can't paint it. You can't because I prayed for a pink house for you. God got it for you. It's pink, just like I asked Him."

Oh, that we dare go to God like Michal Zoe with a child's heart, asking and believing that He will answer our simple and specific prayers. Now, that's faith in The WOW Zone, where walking on water is a way of life and "a little child will lead them."*

*Isaiah 11:6

SUPERHEROS AND JESUS

"Good morning. Did you have any dreams last night?" A question I ask my grandkids from time to time."

"Yes, I did!" 4-year-old grand-twins, Nya and Arin, shouted almost simultaneously.

"Oh, yeah? And what did you dream? Do you remember?"

This time Arin had the jump on Nya (his senior by two minutes) and took control of the conversation. "Yes, Grandma, I remember. I remember."

Nya, Michal Zoe and I anxiously awaited his recollection.

Arin did not disappoint, "I dreamed about Superman and Jesus!"

"What?? Both? In the same dream?" I asked.

"Yes, I saw Superman and I saw Jesus; but…" He appeared a bit befuddled as he reached inside himself for the rest of his dream. He continued, "BUT, they didn't see each other."

"Word?" I offered for his siblings and myself.

Demonstratively, Arin stood up and reenacted portions of his dream.

"Superman was standing here." Like a superhero himself, Arin jumped over to the other side of the dining room and continued, "And, Jesus was over here." With the agility of a 4-year old, he adjusted his stance to the far corner of the room, "But...No, here! Jesus was here. But, Grandma, they didn't see each other."

Nya, Michal Zoe and I looked at each other, trying to put it all together with a glance interpreted as an unspoken, How can that be?

But wait, as if gifted with telepathy, Arin to the rescue, offered his assessment: "Well, I think Superman hasn't met Jesus yet."

"Oh, okay. Maybe they'll meet another night in your dreams," I offered.

As if frozen in the moment, he pondered, then adjusted his cape and said, "Maybe, Grandma. I think so."

Perhaps, out of respect, or unable to top that dream, Nya and Michal Zoe, allowed the flow of the morning to take a turn away from dreams, superheroes and Jesus; and back to the breakfast menu.

Me? My mind seemed tickled and inspired by the limitless possibilities and capacity for faith found in a child's fertile imagination.

WONDER BRA

It all started when I bought an expensive wireless, padded, strapless bra that made me look like I had the breasts of a 25-year old.

On my way home from the store, wearing my new bra, I stopped at my son's to visit my then 23-month old granddaughter, Michal Zoe.

She wanted me to read her a story, so I sat on the couch and as I read, little Michal Zoe nestled in close and rested her head on my bosom.

About half-way through the story, she tweaked my left breast. "Breast, Grandma."

I nodded in agreement. "Yes, baby." I thought that was cute. Being a breastfed child, I figured it only natural for her to know that these were indeed breasts. Grandma's breasts; but breasts none-the-less. I continued reading with the story.

Then, Michal Zoe looked up at me sweetly smiling and tweaked my breast again.

"What are you doing, girl?"

She gave me the widest most mischievous grin, smacked her lips, gave my breast another tweak, and handled it like she was positioning it and herself for something.

She came in close and said, "Yum, Yum, Grandma, Yum, Yum." Suddenly, she dived into my breast like a submarine on full alert.

Periscope down. Dive. Dive.

Stunned and strategically interceding on behalf of my left breast, I scrambled to get up off the soft white leather couch. I was up and away from the evidently confused and hungry Michal Zoe.

"No, Michal Zoe. Stop." She wouldn't stop. I shouted out for reinforcements, "Mike, come get your daughter off me."

"Yum, Yum, Grandma, Yum, Yum. Michal Zoe was undaunted. Her urgent quest for dinner from someone other than her mother continued all the way to the floor as I lost my balance.

"Come on, girl. Back up off me." I was in a fight for my life.

Her father pulled her away.

As I fought to recover, I adjusted my new wonder bra and said, "Girl, you just don't know. If you had got a hold one of these breasts, you'd choke on the dust."

Of course, she didn't understand the comedy in my statement but she saw the joy and heard the laughter, so she laughed too.

Oh, these are the comedies of life that you don't want to miss. Moments on the way to other moments which lead to joy and laughter. Remembering such moments help us get through any storm and reminds us that the joy of the Lord is our strength. (Nehemiah 8:10)

DEAR HEAVENLY FATHER:

Thank you for the moments of comedy in our lives that relieve the stress and give us a clearer perspective on the absurdity of holding onto our fears, doubts, and exasperation—anything that gets in the way of us experiencing the joy of the Lord which is our strength. Help us to laugh off some of the sludge left over from the hard, austere, and tough times.

Thank you so much for these breaks that lighten us and allow us to enjoy the people who populate our lives. And no matter what may be going on inside and outside of us, show us how to develop our sense of humor that keeps us from breaking under the weight of what is not ours to carry. Perhaps laughter reminds us to cast all my cares and burdens onto you. Teach us to smile, laugh, hope, believe, trust, and know that You are in the littlest of details. Amen. So be it!

CHAPTER 5: FAITH HOLDS ON

"Perseverance must finish its work so that you may be
mature and complete, not lacking anything."
James 1:4 (NIV)

TOGETHER

Together

I have a vision.

You have a vision.

When you and I become one,

we will be the totality of THE vision conceived in the mind of God

and given life before we were born.

With longsuffering and grace,

He continually saved us from ourselves

in order to bring us to Himself

and now one to the other.

Together, we will move mountains and men!

FAITH SEES THE UNSEEN

A little boy was in the park flying his kite.

A 7-year-old girl in a purple jacket saw the little boy holding his ball of string and looking up at the sky. She stopped next to him and asked, "What are you doing?"

The little boy, never taking his eyes off the sky, answered, "Flyin' my kite."

She looked at the sky and all she saw were bulging gray clouds. "What kite? I don't see no kite. You're crazy."

With a knowing smile, he calmly looked over at the little girl, "It's up there. I don't have to see it. I know that it's there!"

A bit exasperated, the little girl stretched her neck hoping to get a glimpse of the invisible kite. "Well, I still don't see nothin'. How do you know it's there?"

This time he didn't take his eyes off the sky as he spoke into the air, "I can feel the pull."

How often have I, like the little girl, stretched and strained to see what only the eyes of faith can see—the unseen. And sometimes, like her, if I can't touch it, feel it, or taste it, I'm just as quick to say, "It ain't there and don't try to convince me that it is!"

Doubt clouds my vision.

Unanswerable questions bombard my mind like precisely aimed snowballs. Ominous clouds of bills, jobs that never seem to pay enough, days that don't seem long enough, sleepless nights that never end, wounds from family and friends that take too long to heal, dreams that are slow to bear fruit, flames of hope doused by trickling waters of anxiety, and storms that never seem to cease, all make it difficult for me to see. These temporal things blind me to God's eternal presence and lead me to forget that He is the pull.

Faith sharpens my vision.

Perhaps, like me, you know exactly how it feels to want to see the light at the end of the dark alley and the dawn that is promised to follow our darkest nights. Like the little boy flying his kite, we can stand still, look up and feel God's pull despite what we cannot see.

If we ask, God will help us to feel His pull—every day. The pull of His unconditional Love. The pull of God ordering our every step as we press our way through life. The pull of Him orchestrating the marvelous plans that He alone knows and has for our lives.

Together, we are growing stronger in our faith so that we can stand firm and declare to a hurting world, "We know that God lives because we feel His pull. We are sure of what we hope for and certain of what we do not see."

STRUGGLE

"Do some people struggle more than others? I would love to hear that it is okay for me to be struggling. There seems to be spiritual warfare going on in my life." So read an email I received recently from a young woman. As I responded to her, I couldn't get out of my mind the fact that she is not the only one with that question and those feelings. There are many of us going through, right now. For some of us, it's been so deep for too many months—or so it seems.

As I meditated and asked the Lord for a right-now Word for us, these are the verses that the Holy Spirit brought to my remembrance.

"Simon, Simon, Satan has asked to sift you as wheat. But I have prayed for you, Simon, that your faith may not fail. And when you have turned back, strengthen your brothers." (Luke 22:31-32, New International Version).

So we can replace Simon's name with our own. "(name), Satan has asked..." The key word is ASKED! Satan had to request permission because God is Sovereign. So it was then, Water-Walker. And so it is, now!

We, like Simon, at various times in our lives are sifted as wheat. But, Jesus, says, "I have prayed for you, (name) that your faith may not fail." What makes His Word wonderfully personal and powerful is that Jesus tells us that He foresees that we will make it through—

101

with Him as our helper. Jesus says, "And when you have turned back…" not *IF*…but *WHEN*.

Therefore, there must be a divine purpose in it all and through it all: God's perfect purpose—personal TESTIMONIES, yours and mine—that will "strengthen your brothers and sisters."

Yes, through it all, we gain testimonies that far outweigh the temporary emotional, physical, psychological, and spiritual struggles we may have to endure. We gain testimonies that lead to freedom—our own and others. We gain testimonies drenched in the torrential downpour of God's love, forgiveness, and favor. We achieve testimonies empowered with a Holy Ghost potency that would not be possible without the struggle.

Perhaps, my brothers and sisters, it is possible that the greater the suffering the greater the impact of our ministries.

DIVINE DELAY

A reader, who attended one of my talks, wrote: "I relayed the story of the mouse in your bathroom to my 30-year old daughter (complete with animation, I might add)! I told her that your point of this story was to relay that God is in the smallest areas of our lives. Her reply was, 'Yes, but what about the big areas for which we have prayed and have received no answers?'"

Well, my dear readers, I believe that God answers all prayers. Most often with a *Yes, No,* or *Wait. Yes* and *No*, we're usually clear about. However, when God says, "*Wait*"—now that's a whole 'nother reality show.

If you are anything like me, *Wait* is the most difficult answer to grasp.

I have experienced many *Wait* times, like now, when my life is overflowing with uncertainties and I feel like I'm on the verge of everything, and yet on the precipice of nothing. But even still, God grants me the grace to know that He is in the *wait*.

In the moments when discouragement tries to overshadow God's promises, the Holy Spirit reminds me of stories in the Bible like the woman who had a flow of blood for 12 years! She went to countless doctors whose promising remedies. All of them failed. She endured the wagging tongues of the towns' people taunting her with insults. I'm sure, like you and I, she too experienced waves of discouragement and doubt.

Even still, she pressed her way. Perhaps it was within this incredibly long wait, complete with disappointments that her faith in God increased to the point where she was ready to go where few dared—to Jesus the Christ!

Perhaps that faith first took flight when she heard that Jesus was in town. She got up that morning and went out seeking the only one she had come to believe could heal her. "If only I may touch His garment, I shall be made well," she said to herself."

Maybe she heard the crowd first, or saw the throng of people and wondered, *How will I get to him with all these people around?* But undeterred, she pressed her way and got down on the ground and touched the dusty hem of His garment that tickled the tops of His tired and desert scorched feet.

With no further delays, *Jesus turned and saw her. "Take heart, daughter,"* he said, *"your faith has healed you." And the woman was healed at that moment.* (Matthew 9:20-22, NIV)

THROUGH IT ALL--PERSEVERE!

I once read an intriguing definition for "persevere" in a Bible glossary. *"Perseverance is the ability to endure hardship and suffering without complaining or becoming angry."*

Shall I offer my own inventory of this essential fruit?

I had a long history of trying to circumvent hardship and suffering by whatever means necessary. I opted for the easier, softer thing. "Hard choices were the wrong choices" was my motto. There were so many hard decisions left unmade and the choices I did make— indulging habits, lusts, and envy—were all contrary to everything the Word of God lovingly teaches. I also had a nasty habit of crying, moaning, and complaining at any hint of physical, emotional, and spiritual suffering; I complained even though I must admit that most of the suffering in my life was self-inflicted—even since embracing Jesus Christ as my Lord and Savior.

Where did my inability to persevere get me? So deep into the pits of despair that only a merciful and loving God could have dug me out. Also, my choices always left me short of the marvelous plans that God intended for my life if I yielded to His will and cast all my hopes, cares, and concerns at the foot of the Cross.

And you know what else I found out about myself? Sometimes, like a drowning swimmer who fights the lifeguard that's trying to save her, I have to be knocked out by life in order for God to pull me safely to shore.

However, once I got the Word of God in me and built a personal intimate relationship with God, I saw the necessity to press my way—to persevere. As I learned to keep my spiritual eyes on Jesus, the Holy Spirit imparted His strength and wisdom which allowed me to make the sometimes hard but right choices that propelled me closer to God's perfect will for this life that He so graciously saved.

When I want to give up, and that thought enters my mind sometimes, I don't. There are times when I want to stretch out on the road and cry out, "No more, life is just too hard!" But I've found that along the way somewhere God has changed my mind—my perspective—and I refuse to give up five minutes before the miracle happens.

I have found that when I call upon my Savior, I am given the ability that I could never give myself—no matter how many self-help books I read—to persevere. By the power of the Holy Spirit, I am able to go one more step, cast aside all fear, chase away my doubts, and stomp down the enemy of my soul.

By the Spirit's power, I am able to speak life to my circumstances, command that the raging storm to cease and desist, write one more sentence, seize opportunities, let go the past, forgive myself and forgive the same person yet another time for the same thing I forgave him for the last time. I find that like Paul and Timothy I can do all things through Christ who strengthens me.

If there is ever a glossary in any of the books I write, under "perseverance" there will be a solitary picture—Jesus Christ—nailed to the cross. He was, is, and forever will be—the definition and the example.

A SACRIFICE OF THANKSGIVING

In Corrie ten Boom's autobiography, The Hiding Place, she writes of her and her family's imprisonment in a Nazi concentration camp in Germany for hiding Jews. Once they were rustled off the train, miraculously Corrie and her sister were able to get a wallet-sized Bible pass the murderous guards and into the squalid lice-infested barracks. Every night, exhausted, near starvation, and under the threat of death should they be discovered, Corrie and her sister held a Bible study and shared the good news about Jesus Christ.

Corrie hated the lice and complained to her sister. "Corrie," her sister said, "God has a reason for every living creature's existence; so we must thank Him even for the lice."

Begrudgingly, Corrie heeded her sister's admonishment and began to thank God for the lice during her prayer time. The Bible study continued even after her sister died because of the cruelties she endured at the hands of the Nazi's. Months later, as Corrie was released due to a clerk's mistake, she passed the Bible on to a woman who had become a Christian.

It was later revealed that the Bible study held in secret was never disrupted because of the lice! The guards refused to enter the barracks for fear of being infested by lice.

This story had such an impact on me that a few years ago I resolved to apply this biblical principal of offering a sacrifice of thanksgiving to my faith-walk. While I did not have lice, I lived in a tough neighborhood and had more than my fair share of the District of Columbia's roach population living with me in my apartment.

I worked so hard to get rid of the vermin, but rather than the pesticide annihilating the army of roaches, it acted as an aphrodisiac, and my unwelcome boarders bred a division of reinforcements that seemed determined to cut my life off at the pass.

Feeling like a brand new kind of fool, I decided to kneel ever so carefully and prayed despite the army of roaches around me.

Father God, You know how hard this is for me to thank you for these living creatures that I'd much rather do without. But still, I am willing. OK. Here goes...Thank You for the roaches. I can't believe I'm doing this. I am really getting in touch with the fact that Your ways are far and above my ways. So, I'm trusting that I am right where I'm supposed to be even though you know that I'd rather be further down the line than I am. But nevertheless, thank You for this apartment and everything in it—including the roaches.

And so began my experiment in offering a sacrifice of thanksgiving. Perhaps God had purposes unbeknownst to me. Every day, I prayed a similar prayer always remembering to thank God for the ever-multiplying and ever-present roaches.

While my circumstances didn't change, I noticed that some other things changed—my attitude and perspective on my circumstances. I found that words of gratitude began pouring out of my once begrudging lips.

Most times, during prayer, I wept as I meditated on the changes that were happening within my spirit—the place where I really live. I began to thank God for other obstacles, and the people that I found it difficult to love. I began to believe that He would use all these things and people to strengthen, make and mold me to be more like my Jesus.

Within a few weeks of offering my sacrifices of thanksgiving, God interceded and I was offered a job as a House Manager for a North Carolina transitional shelter for women in recovery from drug addiction. I sold and gave away everything that wouldn't fit into my car and moved to North Carolina—straight into a *roach-free* apartment.

Something else happened later; I was given the opportunity to conduct workshops at public housing developments. I felt a kinship with everyone that attended, mainly because I could empathize with them. I had lived in similar conditions and knew what it was like to cut the lights on during the night and watch the troops of roaches retreat.

I knew what it was like to live with gunfire and helicopters hovering at 3:00 a.m. in search of the thug-of-the night. Through it all, my testimony was made stronger and perhaps more effective by God's grace.

What circumstances, situations, or conditions, are you feeling the least grateful for right now? What are the "roaches" and "lice" in your life? The un-pleasantries of daily life can weigh us down but offering a sacrifice of thanksgiving can lift us up above and beyond what we see and help us to tap into the invisible that makes possible all things.

Your situation is not hopeless! Please don't give up five minutes before the miracle happens.

God is our hope, our very present help in time of trouble and even in our moments of discouragement. But we've got to do something: Draw near to Him and He will draw near to us. We can take our eyes off of the roaches and lice in our lives and fix our eyes on the Maker of Heaven and Earth.

Once Corrie ten Boom was released, she spent the next 30 plus years, until her death, spreading the good news about Jesus around the world. Her message was the message that her dying sister made her promise that she would tell others once she was released, "There is no pit so deep that God's love is not deeper still." People around the world listened to Corrie's message of the Hope that is Jesus because she had endured the lice and every other abhorrent thing that went with it there in the concentration camps of Nazi Germany.

Once we come to believe, like Corrie, that there is nothing that happens or comes into our lives under the sun that has not already been sifted through God's hands then we find that we can live in the fullness of the freedom that only Christ can give. When our sacrifices of thanksgiving waft up to God like sweet smelling incense, He rains down on us blessings-upon-blessings.

I challenge you to offer your sacrifices of thanksgiving for the next seven days. At the end of the seven days, write down your experience, ponder on the changes that you notice, and pass on the principle of a sacrifice of thanksgiving to others.

WELL WORTH THE WAIT

Yes? I love the smell of *Yes* anytime of the day. *No?* I've learned to graciously take a *No* because now I know that God sees way down the line. *Maybe?* On a good day, I've been known to embrace a faith-filled *Maybe*. *Wait?* The hardest-to-endure-word in my psychological, mental, emotional, and spiritual consciousness is **WAIT**.

The only thing that makes wait a concept I can live through is juxtaposing it with God's promises; especially, Isaiah 40:31, "But those who wait on the LORD Shall renew their strength; They shall mount up with wings like eagles, They shall run and not be weary, They shall walk and not faint." I've strode to the rhythm of that verse, using it like a mantra during many a brisk morning walk, determined to get it into my spirit so that I could hold on, trust God, and go on to the next thing at hand.

And now I know that I'm not the only one who has hoped against all odds that a change is gonna come. I believe this is the year when God will grant us some of the greatest desires of our hearts. Long-time hopes. Eternally-flamed dreams.

I believe that because we waited, persevered, held on to God's promises, passed more tests than we fell short of—because we refused to give up hope, or give the enemy of our souls any ground—because we cried out to the Lord when we had no one else to turn to (and even when we did have others to turn we chose the Lord

113

instead) that we have pleased Him. We saw that He made a way. Suddenly—He made a way.

When we felt like quitting, if only for a whisk of a moment and considered lying down on the side of the road, we didn't. Some of us sat down for a minute and caught our breath; but we didn't stay there; we got up in spite of everything that tried to convince us that we were too tired to get up. With the second, third, and fourth wind of the Holy Spirit, we got up and pressed our way.

When all seemed to be against us, we boldly shouted through our tears and groans, "If God be for us who can be against us?" When it looked like defeat was imminent, somehow we felt like going on. We praised God with the eyes of faith for the imminent victories yet unseen and for the triumphs faith assured us were around the bend and one more shovel of hope away. We kept digging.

Yes, we persevered. No, we didn't quit. Maybe, we listened briefly to the whispers of doubts; but God's Word hushed them. And through it all, we waited on God and are better equipped to live out His plans for our lives because of it. God keeps His promises and Jesus stands in the gap for us making sure that absolutely no weapon formed against us prospers.

Thus, we stand here today, clothed in our right minds and with yielded hearts on the verge of realizing some of our greatest desires. We, Chosen Ones, have crossed the threshold of a brand new day and a brand new year—fresh, clean and unused—prepared for us. A new year to live, trust, hope, pray, laugh, prosper, grow, praise, and believe God. This is the year the Lord has made, let us rejoice and be glad in it. WE WILL SEE that it was WELL WORTH THE WAIT!

The promises of God for your life are breaking through! I believe we will just walk right into our breakthroughs so naturally that we will forget the birth pains because what we behold will be so exquisite—far beyond what we could have asked, thought, or imagined.

The past pain will only serve as a spring board on which our awesome testimonies will be launched. And, together, we will continue to overcome, because we will share those testimonies, as the Lord leads—forgetting our insecurities and moving forward boldly in God's Spirit.

We will get in touch with our stories and share them with each another—especially in these last days. It is our responsibility to encourage one another. To let our lights so shine among men that they will see our good works and glorify God in Heaven—that is our destiny. Revelation 12:11 reminds us that we overcome by the blood of the Lamb and the word of our testimony.

Yes, it's all been well worth the wait. It's your time to shine. It's time to shout from the rooftops what God has done for you in the dark. It's your time to mount up with wings like the eagles; to run and not be weary; to walk and not faint.

DEAR HEAVENLY FATHER:

Thank You for hearing and answering our prayers. Thank You that You are greater than the doubts that fill our inner world. As we limp back into our perspective corners at the sounding of life's bells, we ask that You continue to strengthen and refresh us. Please hush the Whispers of Doubt so that we may fight the good fight and finish the race set before us. Continue to surround us with godly counsel that will tell us not what we may want to hear but what we need to hear. Surround us with people who will encourage and uplift us especially during these tough times. With and because of You, the victory is already won! Amen. So be it!

CHAPTER 6: FAITH LETS GO

"Do not be anxious about anything,
but in everything, by prayer and petition,
with thanksgiving, present your requests to God.
And the peace of God,
which transcends all understanding,
will guard your hearts and your minds in Christ Jesus."
Philippians 4:6-7 (NIV)

117

STANICE ANDERSON

TRANSITIONS

Transitions are the hardest to bear
From this to that
From one consciousness to another

The inner construction of it all
The drilling doubts
The paved plans
When you have blueprints of your own

Only to discover it is more cost-effective to yield to God's
right-of-way.

LETTING GO

Letting go is never easy—never.

Ever since I made a decision to turn my life and will over to God's care twenty-five years ago, I have slowly let go of old perspectives, attitudes, and some of the people that populated my life.

Shortly after I had stopped using drugs, a woman who had been my get-high partner, somehow got my telephone number and called me. I knew that I couldn't stay drug-free if I continued to hang out with her.

"Stanice, meet me after work. You know I get paid today."

Hearing her voice coupled with "payday" brought back vivid images of hypodermic needles, and my body slumped with my head bobbing back and forth in a drug-induced stupor. My heart raced as I felt the twinges of agitation that always preceded the anticipation of the thrill of the chase to find the best heroin package on the street. "*God help me*," my prayerful thought zoomed upward like lightning striking in reverse.

Immediately, my mind snapped back to my new drug-free reality. Determined to hold on to my new life free of the despair, degradation, and hopelessness that were a daily part of the addicted lifestyle. I focused on the grace and love of God, the hope I found, my son I had begun to build a relationship with, and my new friends who encouraged me and were willing to teach me how to be all that God had created me to be. I didn't hear much of what my friend said.

Feeling a jolt of heavenly strength, I said, "No, girl. I don't use anymore and you don't have to use anymore either. God can change your life just like He changed mine, if you would only let Him. Why don't you meet me at a twelve-step meeting? Let me introduce you to some people God put in my life who help me not use drugs one day at a time. Just like we got high together? We can stay clean together."

"Okay, girl. What time and where?"

I gave Pat the time and address. That was over 25 years ago. She has yet to meet me at a twelve-step meeting. A couple of times a year, she calls and I invite her to my clean-time celebration but she never comes. I keep praying for her and my hope is that she will make it out of the bondage of addiction—alive.

Letting go is never easy—never.

I also had to learn to let go of old behaviors, especially since I had been such a promiscuous woman—it was part of the lifestyle. I knew that I needed help to change, so I talked it over with my mentor, Dorine Phelps.

"How do I get through the lonely nights alone?"

She looked at me with the tender look of a wise mother. "Baby, you just have to pray, hold one, don't use drugs, and you will start to want something different for yourself."

A few months after trying out my mentor's suggestions, I walked to a party up the street from where I lived. A new friend was giving the party for her cousin, whom I did not know. I danced so much that I needed some fresh air to cool off, so I went out to the backyard. As I looked at the full harvest moon, I softly sang my favorite old song by Smokey Robinson and the Miracles, "Ooo Baby Baby." I was alone or so I thought.

During the second stanza, I heard singing coming from behind me—it was a man's voice.

I slowly turned around, without missing a beat in the song, and my eyes delighted in the most incredibly handsome, smooth-skinned Black man I had seen in a long, long time. The moonlight outlined his silhouette and seemed to make him shimmer. It was like a scene in a romantic comedy. It also reminded me of the commercial where the woman runs in slow motion through a large field of swaying wildflowers toward her man and then jumps into his opened strong arms.

We continued signing our duet, never missing a beat. We finished the song in perfect harmony. When he flashed that perfect smile, I felt like a teenager again.

He said, 'We sounded real good together. What's your name?"

Melodiously I said, "Stanice."

"Stee-niece?" He fought for the right pronunciation.

121

I was used to people mispronouncing my name, so I offered the usual help. "No, Stan-niece. Stan like in Stanley. My dad's name is Stanley. My brother's name is Stanley and my mother's name is Stannette."

"For real?"

"No, I was just kidding about my mother. Her name is Ginny."

It broke the ice and we waded into a conversation.

"I've seen you before. You came to my cousin's celebration a few months ago. I asked her about you. I'd really like to get to know you better. And before you even ask, no I'm not dating anybody. Do you live around here?"

How presumptuous of him, I thought. But still I answered with a simple, "Yes."

"Do you live alone?"

"Yes."

"It's my birthday tonight and I would really like to spend it with you. Why don't we go to your apartment?"

Is that what you usually do on your birthday, go home with a woman you just met?"

He backed up a few steps. "No. It's just you I'm feeling the need to be with. I don't know what it is but I'm just drawn to you."

"I'll tell you what it is. It's lust!" I said. At least it sounded like my voice. I couldn't believe I said that.

"No, you got me all wrong. Don't judge me by other men you may have met. But, hey we can talk about that on the way to your apartment."

"No!" I said it so vehemently that I scared myself.

"Hey, Stan-neice, no problem." He twisted his words in like a knife. "It's your loss."

As he walked away, I wanted to shout out, "*Ask me again.*" But I said nothing. He kept walking and didn't even bother to look back.

Stunned at the way I handled the situation, I stayed looking at the harvest moon and wondered by I felt like I had done something wrong and unnatural. After a few minutes, I went back into the party. I made my way through the crowd and upstairs toward the front door. As I put on my jacket, I wanted to find him and tell him that I had changed m mind but I didn't. Instead, I whispered, "*Lord, let him ask me just one more time, please.*"

I walked slowly down the street toward my apartment, turned occasionally, and hoped to see him running to catch up with me before I made the right turn. It seemed colder going home than it did when I had walked up to the party. The guy never called out and I never heard footsteps or a song from behind. I was alone—again.

One I got home, I prepared for bed and prayed, "God, *please help me get through the night. I am so lonely.*" I cried myself to sleep that night.

Letting go is never easy—never.

The next day I got dressed up in my finest royal blue suit and went to the banquet that I had looked forward to for weeks—alone. This was another exercise suggested by Dorine, about learning how to take myself out and not depend on a man to take me everywhere.

When I walked through the door of the banquet hall, I noticed at a table by the entrance the same incredibly handsome guy from the night before with his arm around a beautiful woman. She was staring up in his face beaming a smile and straightening his tie. He looked at me and lowered his head.

I held my head high and gracefully walked into the main room. Friends ran over to greet me with hugs. They suggested that I join them at their table. As I followed them, I whispered softly, *"Thank you, Lord, for last night 'cause I sure would have felt like a fool today."*

Letting go is never easy—never. But until we let go of the old, we cannot embrace the new.

My mentor once told me, "Girl, when God is ready to bless you—you gonna mess around and miss the blessing because you're all jammed with that." Whatever "that" is for us at any given time in our lives. She's right! Sometimes we hold on so tightly to the old, not realizing that, until we let it go, God can't move us to the next level of our faith-walk.

How can we press forever forward, when we insist on dragging into our present and future what I refer to as "blasts from the past"? Whether these "blasts" are destructive behaviors, harmful relationships, or negative thought patterns, we have to let them go. God stands ready to bless us. He wants to do a new thing in our lives, if we are willing to let go of the old.

How can we know what God's marvelous plan for our life is, if we are busy trying to work out our own plans? Why not surrender our plan to God by asking Him. "What is your plan for my life that you predestined even before I was born?" Trust God and let Him show you your uniqueness in Him. There is something that only you were born to bring to the world. Let go of your preconceived notions of what that may be and allow God to bring to fruition His glorious plan for your life that is far greater than anything that you could think, ask, or imagine.

Fall back into the arms of God. Trust and don't be afraid.

EMPOWERED BY FAITH

Although I've been born-again and on-fire-for-Jesus since February 1984 and delivered from a vicious and devastating drug addiction since May 20, 1985, it was in the wee hours of July 29, 2001 that I smoked my last cigarette.

My smoke-free life began by thanking God for setting me free from the bondage to cigarettes—while I was still smoking. Every time I went to the store to buy cigarettes, I visualized a smoke-free me and thanked God that one day it would be as I pictured it in my mind. Empowered by faith, I called what was not as if it already was.

I prayed for a quit date. Later that week, the answer—July 29th, 12:01 a.m.—floated into my mind and overpowered every other thought.

In preparation for my last days as a smoker, I bought a carton of cigarettes. I chained smoked until one minute before midnight July 28th. With the last cigarette extinguished, I prayed, "Please, help me Holy Spirit to do WITH you what I cannot seem to do without you—stop smoking and stay stopped." I crumbled the remaining cigarettes, threw them into the toilet, and flushed. I watched the swirling clumps of tobacco and filters disappear out of my life.

With mustard-seed faith and up-stretched arms, I reached toward The Throne Room of God and pulled down my new smoke-free life like a ripe pear plucked from a tree.

The first three days were HELLISH. Each time an urge to smoke grabbed me by the throat; I paced, prayed, and thanked God for each second that I did not light a cigarette. The urges subsided but always returned. The grueling process reminded me of the first few weeks some eighteen years prior when God delivered me from a heroin habit.

On day four, while feverishly cleaning my house to keep my hands occupied, I came across a small, white, plastic bottle of bubble solution that guests were given at a friend's wedding. I went outside on my front porch and blew bubbles through the tiny wand. It was as close to smoking as I could get.

I watched the iridescent spheres rise, fall, and pop in the heat of the summer sun. I felt like a child again. It reminded me of simpler times and innocent days before addictions and the rooted emotional pain that proved itself fertile ground for them all. My times on the front porch increased to include sticky summer nights and dew-glistened dawns.

One evening, a neighbor shouted from across the street, "Ms. Anderson what's with the bubbles?"

"The Lord delivered me from cigarettes! Now, I'm blowing bubbles for Jesus!"

He laughed and offered an encouraging, "Good for you!"

By the end of my first smoke-free week, in addition to blowing bubbles, I puffed yellow No. 2 pencils. However, it drew too much attention so a classier alternative entered my mind—clear, plastic drinking straws that I got from fast food restaurants. I cut them in half and puffed. These were especially helpful when I drove, as driving and smoking seemed one activity. It amazed me how robotically I operated when it came to my smoking rituals, including at work.

I worked for USA TODAY in an office on the 22nd floor. More times than I wish to confess, I rode the elevator down to the subbasement. I walked through the double-glass doors that spilled into the designated smoking area, greeted by the putrid stench of abandoned cigarette butts like thousands of times before. Each time like instant replay stuck on repeat, the same admonishment kidnapped my brain, *Why are you here? You don't smoke anymore!*

Sheepishly, I walked back to the elevator, and silently prayed my way to the 22nd floor. On one of those trips, I realized that through the years, I cheated employers out of *work* time. Time that I spent smoking. There were also many times at restaurants that I forgot I no longer smoked. Either I found myself awkwardly rescinding requests for *smoking* seating or I went outside after meals because tar and nicotine had replaced traditional desserts.

Temptations to smoke lurked everywhere like thieves behind bushes. Trails of smoke followed me to my car. I zeroed in on every movie and TV character that smoked. My cigarette brand distributed *buy one, get one free* coupons right to my mailbox.

Telephone conversations shortened and my nerve endings seemed to fire mishaps if I talked too long without a cigarette. Sleep and food were modes of escape. Scared that I couldn't live smoke-free, I prayed, *Lord, I'm not doing so good. Help me.*

Later that day, my son, Mike, telephoned me. "What are you doing?"

"Nothing much, Son."

"Moms, you still not smoking?"

"Yeah, but just barely."

"You're doing good, though, Moms. I'm thinking about coming over to see you."

"Sure, Mike. Come on. I could use a visit from you right about now."

About a half-hour later, he arrived at my house.

I hugged him, "So good to see you. What's up?"

"Mom, I just wanted to smell you."

"What? Smell me?"

"Yep. Do you realize that in my entire twenty-five years on this earth I have never smelled you NOT smelling like nicotine?"

"Oh, my God. No, I never thought about it. I'm so selfish. I'm sorry."

We hugged. I sensed his joy. He sensed my sadness.

"It's okay," he assured me. "Bottom line, you are no longer a smoker."

My son and I chilled together that day—not doing much of anything but enjoying the best thing—being together. I stole away for a few moments, closed my eyes, held my head and my hands to the sky, and prayed, "Thank you. Now, I can't turn around."

My son's purposeful visit sealed my destiny as a smoke-free woman. Our actions and words were locked together in heavenly places and the generational curse broken.

Now all these years later, my son's children, five-year-old Michal Zoe, and the three-year-old twins, Arin and Nya, have never smelled their GrandMa-Ma smelling like nicotine.

Perhaps, you struggle with cigarettes (or some other addiction—nasty habit—or counterproductive behavior). Do yourself a favor—take the struggle off yourself and put it on God. Lay that burden and all your burdens at the foot of The Cross. Say these words, "God, I've tried it my way and to this day it has not worked. I can't do it!

However, this woman, Stanice, reminded me today that YOU CAN. Please do for me what you've done for her. Take the taste out of my mouth, out of my spirit, out of my life—for good. Help me to step into my preordained destiny. With you, God, nothing is impossible. Set me free from this bondage to (whatever). Surround me with supportive family and friends, perhaps some I have yet to meet, so that I can stay free—one day at a time. Amen. So be it!

You know, the battle has already been fought and won! Jesus is the Victor and we have the victory through Him. Empowered by faith, reach up and snatch your newly assigned freedom from the throne room of God like ripe pears plucked from a tree.

THE ART OF LETTING GO

Perhaps like me, God has been teaching you the art of letting go. Letting go of the old in order to embrace the new. Letting go of what is not working so that He can bring to me what is. Letting go of trying to fix it or work it out on my own...and letting Him bring His perfect will and plans into my life.

Letting go of the old ideas that are not based on THE living WORD of God but soul-draining stuff grafted on my mind over years of listening to what the world has to say...simply because what God has to say is contrary to the lies I've been bombarded with all my life. Lies and misconceptions like from the poem, *Invictus*, by William Ernest Henley, which I had to learn in high school, "I am the master of my fate the captain of my soul."

Then ushered in by the Madison Avenue ad agencies was the *me generation*. The world instructed me to look into the mirror and repeat affirmations like, "it's all about me and my inner child." And let's not forget the golden-arched message "you deserve a break today."

What I deserved was death by inverted crucifixion but what I got was God's unmerited favor! He sent his only son, Christ Jesus, to die on the cross for me and my sins; so that I could have life and that more abundantly.

I'll be honest with you. It would be extremely difficult for you to pry my "only" cup of coffee out of my grasp; even at the expense of 3rd degree burns on my hands. Give up my only son? Any son? Any child? For anybody? Unthinkable! No way, ever!

Yes, letting go of the hype and replacing it with God's truths. Letting go of the bitterness—so that He can replace it with His Love. Letting go of the anger—so that He can replace it with His peace that surpasses all human understanding—especially mine. (Philippians 4:7)

Letting go of the plans and dreams that I have for myself or allowed others to force-feed me—so that He can orchestrate into my life His perfect plans prepared long before I was born. (Jeremiah 29:11-13)

Letting go of the fear-based procrastination and instead embracing the life and reality of God's words, "For God has not given us a spirit of fear, but of power and of love and of a sound mind." (2nd Timothy 1:5)

Letting go of all that's broken in my life— relationships—emotions—ideas—concepts—beliefs about myself and others.

Letting go of the burdens, frustrations, and hopelessness, trying to understand the profundities of life— when His ways are so far and above our ways and His thoughts higher than our thoughts could ever hope to be. (Isaiah 55:9) Letting it all go!

The most viable and empowering solution eludes me like my own shadow in the blazing afternoon sun— Free-Falling back into the all-powerful and loving arms of

God and RESTING. Resting like David who in Psalm 131 wrote, "I have stilled and quieted my soul; like a weaned child with its mother, like a weaned child is my soul within me." (Psalm 131:2)

NEVER TO RETURN

There's a cold chill in the air now.
The trees have been stripped of their garments of green.

The first snow of winter has been raped of its whiteness
And is now only polluted slush.
Amidst this stands a lonely woman.

Deaf to the sounds that fill the brisk city air.
Blind to the passing crowd hurrying to the warmth of
destinations only they know.

She is thinking of the years gone by
The years that no King's treasures can ever return
The years of romp and play, the years of love and let go.
A tear softly trickles down her cold face onto the
mutilated snow

A gentle uncertain smile loosens her lips
She closes her eyes and reminisces.
She is thinking of the years gone by

The hopeful and carefree years, the fat and fruitful years.
The years that brought no evidence of the loneliness that
was yet to come.

She is thinking of the roller coaster rides at Coney Island,
Summer camp, the Senior Prom, her first kiss, her
wedding day.

The cool and tranquil evenings on the beach with the sand
tickling her naked toes.
The gentle breezes touching her face and mind,
Bringing peace and contentment unlike any known
before.

She smiles a sad but hopeful smile
And walks away
Never to return.

Have you let go? Sometimes, it's a one day at a
time kind of thing. Fresh situations and circumstances
equals fresh surrenders. I don't know about you, but I
don't want to be so jammed up with the old that I have no
room for the new.

DEAR HEAVENLY FATHER:

Thank you for giving us the strength and wisdom that we need to let go of the harmful behaviors, people, and ideas. Letting go is not easy for us but with You we can do all things. Help us develop a closer walk with you. Talk us through the lonely nights and days until You populate our lives with positive people. Remind us that we may be lonely but we need never be alone because You are forever with us. Amen. So be it!

CHAPTER 7: FAITH HOPES

"God says, 'I alone know the plans I have for your life;
plans for prosperity and not disaster,
plans to give you a future and a hope'".
Jeremiah 29:11-14 (NIV)

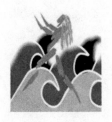

STANICE ANDERSON

ON DAYS LIKE THESE

On days like these,
the dream seems so big
and the resources so few
and the confidence so null and void.

On days like these,
the Holy Spirit reminds me
that the cattle on a thousand hills
are God's--just as I am.
The Lord is my Shepherd,
I shall not want...

On days like these.
I pray pass the circumstances
and rest in the pastures of faith.
The Lord is my Shepherd,
I shall not want...
on days like these…
on days like these.

From Stanice Anderson's One-Woman Show, *Walking On Water
When The Ground Ain't Enuf.*

EXPECTANT HOPE

One of the most powerful verses of scripture in God's love letter to us is Hebrews 11:1, "Now faith is being sure of what we hope for and certain of what we do not see."

Hope is defined as "a wish or desire accompanied by confident expectation of its fulfillment."

Expect is defined, "To look forward to the probable occurrence or appearance of: expecting a telephone call; expects rain on Sunday. b. To consider likely or certain: expect to see them soon."

I am learning that even when all hell seems to break loose in my life, hope is available to me that is never deferred, faith that is immovable, and expectancy that propels me forever forward.

Though sometimes crying out to the Lord in a shower; it is impossible to tell where the stream of water begins and my tears end, STILL I set my mind, like flint, to wait it out, listen, and trust God. In my 25 years since asking Jesus to be Lord of my life, He has never failed to reveal the rose that is hidden from my faith's view; covered in the mud of my humanity and the thorns of what I hope are the last vestiges of my disbelief.

Yet, though my promise land eludes me and the countless cross roads seem more than I can bear. STILL I wield my sword etched with the Word, "Now faith is being sure of what we hope for and certain of what we do not see."

I prophesize to myself, it's imminent. Your breakthrough is a blink and less than a wink away! Don't give up five minutes before the miracle happens. Press on!

The guardian and ministering angels surrounding me declare the round mine as my steadfast hope in God rips a hole in the night and turns it into day. The battle won; I stand expectant and ready to receive the fulfillment of all God promised.

A HOPE NEVER DEFERRED

In a recent dream, I saw lions walking leisurely through the streets of a city. The people seemed oblivious to the imminent danger that was around every corner. Boldly, steadily, the lions advanced, watched, and awaited an opportune moment to pounce upon unsuspecting prey. Fear gripped me spit-less.

Afraid, I ran, sought shelter, and at first said nothing—alerted no one. But then, something greater moved in my spirit and it became clear that I must yell out for all to hear, "Lions in the city. There are lions in the city."

I knocked on people's doors. Some people let me in, some didn't. I warned them, anyway, loudly, through unopened doors. "There are lions in the city."

Later in the dream, I saw my pastor and childhood friend, Omie. She ran alongside me. Homes that heeded the warning, she simply said, "Blessings and peace be on this place." If the door was not opened and the words not heeded she said, "We shake the dust off our feet here." And then, alone again, I ran and shouted, "Lions in the city. There are lions in the city."

There was another strange occurrence in the dream. When the lions and lionesses got so close to me, I felt their hot breath on my arm and leg—they passed by without a growl or any other aggressive behavior. It was as if I were invisible to them. After each lion passed by me, I looked back at them as they swaggered away with tails in motion; but they didn't bother to look at me.

About one week after this dream, things went the makings of a long-awaited Hallelujah-Praise-God-Breakthrough to all-hell-broke-loose-demon-skeet-shoot with me as the target.

My finances went from bad to it-can't-get-worse-than this. And then it did. My boss on my new two-week-old job called me about 7:00 a.m. and announced, "Don't bother coming back to work. It's not working out. The timing's not right."

It was also the day, I had to begin moving out of my apartment that I could no longer afford. Harder still? Examining myself and determining the part I played in it ALL.

As confirmation of my findings, I asked God to use those closest to me to help with my inward journey. My mentor, Dorine, told me long ago, "Sometimes, other people see you better than you see yourself."

This necessary component of my process was painful; but I processed the information as best I could and took it all to my prayer closet. To name a few of the glaring defects that looked back at me from the mirror. I asked God to forgive me for being undisciplined with my money, as well as stubborn. I also asked for whatever I needed to get back on His track for my life.

I would be lost without my intimate and personal relationship with God through Jesus Christ. It has been my lifeline and The Holy Spirit has been my saline drip. During days like these, when I am at my weakest, I feel His comfort the strongest. It's as if He wraps His loving, warm liquid arms around me and whispers, "For I know the plans I have for you, plans to prosper you and not to harm you, plans to give you hope and a future." (Jeremiah 29:11)

Hope is defined as "a wish or desire accompanied by confident expectation of its fulfillment." God is the ever present hope that is immutable and never deferred.

Perhaps you are going through trials or otherwise hard and painful situations and circumstances. Perhaps you are faced with yourself and you don't like what you see. Perhaps there are decisions that you have made or not made in your life that you find it hard to live with. The feelings, fears, mistakes, and doubts though sheltered from others as they may be—they are there.

You know it and God knows it.

And I know this—YOU are not alone in what I call "the sometimes-I-go-there-dark-place." But WE don't stay in that dark place.

I've been a born-again, on-fire-for-Jesus Christian for 23 years and STILL there are days that I go there; but

God has surrounded me with people that won't let me stay there. People who love God and me enough to tell me the truth. People who remind me that God uses imperfect people like me—STILL.

Plus, God spiritual truths backed by the ageless fact that He loved me—US—so much that He gave His only Son for us so that we may have abundant life and not perish. And He loves us enough to warn and strengthen us, in our dreams and confirm it in His Word, if we ask.

There are lions in the city, indeed.

"Be self-controlled and alert. Your enemy the devil prowls around like a roaring lion looking for someone to devour. Resist him, standing firm in the faith, because you know that your brothers throughout the world are undergoing the same kind of sufferings. And the God of all grace, who called you to his eternal glory in Christ, after you have suffered a little while, will himself restore you and make you strong, firm and steadfast." (1 Peter 5:8-11 NIV)

The problems, trials, challenges, self-created or otherwise, are all distractions to get us off-point so that we are rendered unable to fulfill God's purposes for our lives. It is our faith that is being tested.

Since we know that God works all things together for the good of those who love him and are called according to His purposes (Romans 8:28), He will use the distractions, too, as part of our breakthrough.

Our journeys are charted and God is ordering our steps; going behind, before and ahead of us. He is omniscient and omnipresent far beyond our finite understanding.

I don't understand my journey most days and some days, my mind is not my friend. It tries to convince me that I'm not as far up or down the road as I'm supposed to be.

If I had it my way, I'd be living off the shore of the Caribbean Sea during the winters and the Atlantic Coast during the other three seasons. I would be signing my seventh book by a major publishing house; and my one-woman show, *Walking On Water When The Ground Ain't Enuf*, would be on Broadway—back by popular demand. Both coastal homes would be paid off.

Tomorrow morning, I'd go to the bank for a cashier's check to pay off my son's mortgage; instead I'm living in my son's basement.

And yet, according to the Bible in James 1:9, I got it going on! "The brother in humble circumstances ought to take pride in his high position."

So I'll remind myself AGAIN. Speak a prophetic word to myself AGAIN. *Let go, let God, and praise your all the way through to yet another testimony, you blessed Water-Walker you! God's extreme favor saturates your life. Now, walk like you know that!*

LIVING IN ANSWERED PRAYERS

I'm awake in my dream. Living it, loving it. Dancing in it, resting in it. Thanking God for it. Asking for abundant blessings for those who took the time to pray for me, encourage, inspire, and made sacrifices for me. Those who rocked with me, cried with me, laughed with me, assured me when I wanted to give up, "Gurrll, it's gonna be all right!"

Living in answered prayers. Awake in my dream; knowing that it will never end; but get more real by the day. And when I see Jesus face-to-face, I'll probably fall down on my brand new see-through imperishable knees, mute with words I wish I could say swirling around God's throne like snowflakes hitching a ride on the wind.

I'm awake in my dream! It's in no Marvin Gaye *distant-lover* promise nor is it a *sweet-potato-pie-in-the-sky* place. It's not a *moving-on-up-to-the-eastside thing* nor is it *West Side Story* longing to be retold in 3-D.

I'm awake in my dream. Living in answered prayers. It's here and now. All those tears, emotional pain, disappointments, the feel-like-giving-up and sitting-on-the-side-of-the-road times. The obsessive urgency to be somewhere other than where I am at any given time-- when I don't need to be anywhere but where I am--Living in answered prayers.

"Nobody hears me," I said as I rambled on about what I hoped to do for God in an unidentifiable timeframe, my beautiful dark and relaxed friend, interrupted my train-wrecked thoughts.

"You don't seem to understand. You talk about all you want to do, complain about what you haven't done, what you don't have, the bestsellers you haven't written; but can't you see I am the words of your books and the notes of your song. Me, as well as the many other women that you've mentored through the years. You helped us stay clean and sober one day at a time. I know I, for one, came to a personal relationship with Christ because of you sharing your testimony and faith with me. You listened to me, cried with me, laughed with me, prayed with me, encouraged, and inspired me. We are your music, books, plays, poetry—your friends and God is your rhythm."

And so the stardust fell from my eyes and I saw for the first time that I was, indeed, living in answered prayers. Awake in my dream.

Here and now, I remember the prayers I said for me and I know that others prayed for me. *Lord, help me not to use drugs today. Help me get through one more day.* Clean 24 years come May 20th. Sitting on the side of the bed looking at the Travel Channel, *"Lord, I would love to see some of the fjords of Norway, a sunset while on some pink sandy beach along the Caribbean Sea.*

For years now, traveling, speaking, singing, performing, and spending time with family and friends.

Lord I am desperate, alone, and sick of myself.

Now, I have an intimate and personal relationship with God and myself.

Lord, please restore what the canker worm ate--my relationship with my son, my parents and others who care about me.

I'm blessed with an astounding relationship with my son and mother.

Lord, bless the grandchildren I will have someday. Help me be there for them like I wasn't for my son.

Now, years later, three healthy grandkids who love being with me and I with them.

Lord, help me hone my writing skills and show me what to write. Should I take music lessons at that studio I passed by yesterday?

Now, a published author of a three books and counting. Though slower than some of my peers, but being published none-the-less; performing and singing in my own one-woman show.

Lord, grant me more opportunities to share my story.

Now, contributing author of a major anthology, writer of The WOW Zone inspirational newsletter, host of an internet radio show, writing articles and being interviewed by magazines, radio, and television. Incredible God-granted opportunities!

Lord, please let this biopsy be benign.

It was benign. Though I have health challenges, I'm blessed with great health, a future, hopes and *nothing-but-the-grace-and-mercy-of-God* testimonies.

I'm living in answered prayers.

So what, I'm not rich—yet. So what, I don't have a condo at the ocean—yet. So what, I don't have that Lexus sport drop top. So what, my car is 10 years old, and I have to lay hands on it every other day; it's paid for, gets me and others where we need to go, and I recently met an awesome and reasonable mechanic.

I'd rather not have what I want—with God; then to have everything I want and more—without God. So, I will trust because I know that God is in the *wait*.

He is the *wait* of yet-to-be-answered prayers. Answers that only He knows when I'll be ready to receive.

I have what money can't buy, including incredibly gifted, loving, compassionate, and motivated people that God populates my life with. People who have showed me how to live my dreams in the waking hours--content with much or little and at peace as I drift off to sleep understanding how RICH I really am.

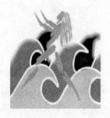

How about you? Are you living in answered prayers? Take a moment. Don't answer prematurely. Ask God to show you.

Look back over your life. Do you have not one— but many testimonies? Is the slumber dust out of your eyes and you're finding yourself living in answered prayers?

LIFE-CHANGING

The sky at 7:10 a.m. on this Tuesday, December 23 2003
is breathtaking.
Cloud patches of shimmering neon pink dots the blue-
gray pallet of sky.

A lone airplane in the far distance appears
like a black ant that lost its' way from the colony.
This pales in comparison to son's news yesterday.
     I am to be a grandmother.
        His life-changing announcement
makes a dreaded Monday of another mundane work week
 seem like the Friday before a three-day holiday weekend.

My mind can hardly contain the flurry of possibilities and
prayers for my first grandchild.

I find myself confused as to what day it really is.
     Monday? Friday Night? The 4th of July?

A moment of clarity steals softly into my consciousness,
as I look at the red-lit numbers of my alarm clock on my
nightstand.
There are only three minutes left of a Monday that I will
never forget.
I have to get up at 4:30 a.m. to get ready for work.
     So...
         Reluctantly,
         I crawl into bed and let the day end.

MORE THAN A WONDER

Grandchildren
Generations of genes on both sides are there—
as with you,
as with me.
It's amazing isn't it?

The creative power of God.

It's like He loves us so much,
that he wants to perpetuate us here on earth as well as in
Heaven.

Us, there with Him—
eventually—
with new immortal bodies that will never wear out
AND remnants of us,
here.

GRAND-MA

While spending the evening with my son and his family, I gave my granddaughter a vocabulary lesson. Two days into being ten-months-old, we worked on our soon-to-be almost-favorite word, "GrandMa." She sat on my lap and studied my lips, as I pronounced clearly, slowly, and repetitively, "Grand-Ma, Grand-Ma."

Michal Zoe peered intently into my mouth, touched my lips, and fluttered her eyes as my breath escaped upon each syllable. She smiled at me in between my long string of the unfamiliar word, as if it registered in some newly discovered corner of her brain. Again, I repeated, "Grand-Ma" until something clicked within both of us and we knew the day's vocabulary lesson was over.

Michal Zoe confirmed this as she slid off my lap and onto the blue-gray carpet. She crawled over to her Mommy and pulled up as if she intended to share her experience in GrandMa's class.

It's okay, I thought, one day she will say "GrandMa" and so much more. I sighed as I let go and yielded to God's perfect timing.

I felt happy and content as I watched her. In the next moment it happened. My granddaughter turned toward me. Distinctly and slowly, she formed her lips and said, "Grand-Ma." As if she knew she aced an exam, she offered Grand-Ma a smile that sealed the day into the annals of our family's history of firsts.

How much more do I, like Michal Zoe want to please my Heavenly Father? And far more joy does He have for us when we please Him.

YOUR VOICE

Your voice
on that cool, breezy, orange leaf-swirled day long ago on
the Fayetteville State University campus.
Mmmm.
I walked slower.
      Slower still.

I zeroed in on your baritone voice
with its southern twang and raspy edges
long before you turned and I saw your face.
Though your smile was quite impressive,
Your vocal chords must have been touched
by angels' fingers;
      While you were in your mother's womb.

Your voice
stirred my soul and roused
my heart from a bad relationship-induced coma.

Your voice
Eagerly announced
to a cold-austere city-beaten me,
in home-grown sincerity,
      Yes, real love is possible;
      And
      I AM its roots.

LOVE IS

Love is
One Total aspect of your being finally uncovered,
discovered,
conquered.

Love is
Behind our masks of hate
Our masks of jealousy
Our masks of deceit.

Love is
you, Love is me.
An epic left unproclaimed
An hour left unmeasured.
Love IS.

WHEN THE STUDENT IS READY

Hello, Chosen One.

Hello

So what's on your mind today?

You and only you—for a change.

Yeah? What about me?

How good you've been to me.

I love you and I'm pleased with you.

But the good I want to do I don't do and what I don't want to do I do.

No matter. I love you now no less than I will love you when you do what you want to do and don't do what you want to do. I've got that kind of love. So what else is on your mind?

Well, all that I've been through; everything I have ever experienced, you are using it and making me look pretty good. Like I know something. Folks don't seem to realize that all I really know is You. It's Your Spirit that's been running most of the show. When I yield that is. Which hasn't been easy; getting to get me to that point, huh?

Yeah, you're special all right.

So Teacher, I got a lot of thanksgiving on the brain lately.

Well that's a good thing. Some folk never say thank you. Remember the 10 lepers, Jesus healed. Only one came back to say, "Thank you."

You know Teacher, I'm really grateful that you got my creative juices a' flowing to write this book. Never in my wildest dreams would I have believed something like this was possible for me.

And never in your wildest dreams would it have been possible without me; but you know that too, don't you?

Yes. I do remember my life without you. And I'll be honest with you, as if I could be otherwise; I'd rather be in living in an alley in Calcutta with you then in a presidential palace without you.

Which is why I chose you, before you were in your mother's womb, I knew your heart. All your experiences—and the ones to come—were and are necessary to get you to the pure essence of why I created you.

My, My.

Everything you are? I birthed into you. I know all, see all, and am in all. Your journey has revealed to you that I AM THAT I AM. The plans for your life—I alone know. I know what you need to live my plans.

Your ways are far and above mine. Trying to grasp your concepts makes me feel woozy. The magnitude of it all.

160

And what a great place for you to be. You have learned just where your strength and hope lie. You know that without me you are nothing and with me all things are possible.

Oh, I love you; but you know all things.

Now, you are ready for the next level in me. Come, sit, listen, and learn, while I teach you marvelous things you know nothing about.

DEAR HEAVENLY FATHER:

We come to You today knowing that You love hearing from Your children. We want to say that we love and adore You, worship and praise You because You alone are worthy. Thank You for Your Word which comforts us, instructs us, reminds us that You know all things and that You orchestrate our lives in such a way that everything we need to have, see, and be rests in You to make available to us.

How wonderful it is to know that even before we were born, You already had plans for our lives—to give us a future and a hope. We surrender to the magnificent thoughts that are cocooned in Your limitless love for us—straining for us to believe.

As Your Word seeps through, soaks, and anoints our souls and spirits, we are being renewed, darkness is fading, and hope gushes forth like oil from a freshly tapped well. For this and all things, we thank You. Amen. So be it!

CHAPTER 8: FAITH BELIEVES

*"But without faith it is impossible to please Him,
for he who comes to God must believe that He is, And that
He is a rewarder of those who diligently seek Him."*
Hebrews 11:6 (NKJV)

LEAPING OVER RAINBOWS

I leap over rainbows using pole vaults of faith.
Contrary to man's myth, the pot of gold is not at the end
of the rainbow; but is found somewhere between the leap
and the silent soar to the other side.

A pot of gold is a fools' prize.
But believing that you can surrender your fears, leave the
surety of the ground, and leap into the unknown knowing
that the all-knowing and living God is with you in the
leap
and waiting for you in the landing,
simultaneously,
is the reward for those who dare
to take God at His Word.

from Stanice Anderson's One-Woman Show, *Walking On Water
When The Ground Ain't Enuf.*

BEAUTY

Once upon a time not so long ago, Beauty eluded me. I'd try to catch a glimpse of beauty in the mirror, but before I could wrap my mind around it.

♫ *Like smoke from a cigarette, it's fading away. Fading away, fading away. Like the feeling we used to get, whenever our lips met.* ♫*

Like fresh and exciting thoughts that tickled my newly awakened mind, Beauty evaded capture like butterflies from hole-ridden nets.

It was so vivid whilst I lay but by the time my feet hit the floor with mirror in my hand, the possibilities and probabilities melted one into the other and became like vapors suspended in the air.

"There's no place like home. There's no place like home," the thoughts taunted.

Then trailed off into nothingness—desiring rather to remain hidden somewhere between sleep and awake under the cloak of a dream.

♫ *The plans we were making for our never breaking up. Like dreams when you're waking up, are fading away. Fading away, fading away.* ♫

Beauty. I wanted it. I needed it.

Aunt Carol said, "It's yours for the looking."

Say it loud, I'm black and I'm proud. Say it loud, I'm black,

I'm black, I never liked that fact, I'm black—so get back.

Step on the crack, you break yo momma's back, step on the line, your daddy drinks wine.

And me?

Pass the black beauties, sticks of weed laced with angel dust, bumpers of beer, with syringes of heroin on the side.

Can't you see? It's one rape too late for me?

One brutal beating too many.

One sodomized moment that was way too much.

One abortion then another that sucked my babies right out of me along with my will to live.

With each dark secret, I got uglier still.

It was more than the straw that broke more than my back.

Call it comeuppance. Call it bad karma. Call it sin. Label it shame.

Call it ♫ *down came the rain and washed the spider out.*♫

Call it obscene!

♫ *It hurts me to think about, how love where there was no doubt. Like a cloud when the sun comes out, it's fading away. Fading away, fading away.* ♫

I've been poured like molten silver through the fiery fingers of God.

Cooled by His breath, shaped by His hand, and rescued from the catacombs of post-traumatic memories.

God extracted the essence of beauty from the ashes and tears.

He restored what the locust ate throughout those dark years.

My name is Beauty and I cannot be snatched from God's Hand.

Low self-esteem seems to be what too many of us try to rise above or learn to live with. Perhaps, if we esteem God more highly, it will matter more what He thinks of us than what we think of ourselves.

In Psalm 139:14 David writes, "I praise you because I am fearfully and wonderfully made; your works are wonderful, I know that full well." What confidence, not in himself but in God. God so loved the thought of you that He breathed you into being.

* Fading Away as sung by The Temptation.

DELAY IS NOT DENIAL

"Delay is not denial," my agent said as she assured me that she had not forgotten my manuscript or me. It had been three LONG months since the work was finished, and I ached for publication details. Almost seven months later, her words were more than a haunting hope. They reminded that in God's time, not mine, more will be revealed.

The delay taught me to walk by faith and not by natural sight. Therefore, with the eyes of my faith, I saw the book. I felt the raised letters of the title spanned across the glossy cover. I smelled the fresh-inked pages. I saw myself at the podium of a packed auditorium as I read from sections bookmarked with neon-pink Post-its peeping over the pages. I experienced the "not yet" as if it already "was." Perhaps spiritual vision is sharpened in the delay.

After we have done our part, we turn all else over to God and stand on His promises while we wait for the results that He alone can orchestrate. His Word reminds us, "... though it tarry, wait for it; because it will surely come."

In this moment, perhaps God is saying to us: "Don't run ahead of me. I AM the Author and the Finisher of your faith. I AM in your past, present and future. My timing is always perfect. In the meantime, trust me and go on to the next thing of your life. When you least expect, I will reveal my perfect will that is immeasurably more than you could ever ask, think or imagine—Creator made just for you. Don't curse the delay! I reside in the delay."

DEAR HEAVENLY FATHER,

We acknowledge that you are still on the Throne. It is you who go before, with and ahead-working together all things for the good of us who love you and are called according to your purpose. Today, we cast our feeble efforts and looming anxieties at the foot of your Throne. In Jesus' name we pray, Amen. So be it!

FRIENDS IN HIGH PLACES

It seems more like writing chose me, rang my number,
and I answered.
Thank God! I had call-waiting.
"Hello? Yes, it's me.
What pig poem? 4th grade?
Oh, that poem, My Trip to Beltsville Farm.
Don't remind me.
Yeah, right, it was good.

How did you get my number anyway?
Oh, friends in high places, huh?

Nalunga, My Beautiful Black Prince?
Yes, I wrote that too.
It was my Black-and-I'm-proud stage.
Afro-sheened, platform heels, black wet-look dress,
and a man finer than Superfly ever hoped to be.
That's right he chose me!
I had to write about how wonderful it felt.
Colored and Negro were out—
Black was in—no more pig poems for me.
I became a vegetarian to prove beyond a shadow of any
doubt that I was a poet
ready to rise up from the cotton fields and fly, fly away.

And then somehow, one day or another, I got caught up
on a trail of marijuana smoke.
Unlike Dorothy and Toto, I landed in a needle-strewn
alley drowning in my own puke.

Yes, I wrote about that too—had no choice.
It was die or write.
Writing was all I had left to pawn for better-days-are-
coming, if-I-don't-die-first dreams.

Write a book? You done gone and lost your mind.
No disrespect intended—'cause you sure do know a lot
about me.

Who did you say gave you my number?
Oh. Right. You got friends in high places.

Yeah, well I got errands to run, a son to pick up, a house
to clean and…
Stories to tell? Books to write? You trippin'!
To this day, I remember what my college professor said,
"You didn't write this story—it's too good.
After all, you're a first-semester freshman."
And he was just a…
Well, that was a long time ago. Yeah, I know. Let it go,
let it go.

Pain and suffering yields words far beyond your years,
the sum of many realized fears,
and the kind of joy that's only birthed through tears.

Where did you get my number?
Right, you got friends in high places.

REALITIES AND DREAMS

Perhaps our hopes are so deeply embedded in the fabric of our souls that they first become realities in our dreams.

In recent dreams, I watched myself, as if in an out-of-body experience being escorted to a huge prison. My tasks included reading my stories and sharing my testimony. In the midst of the sharing, I watched as flaps of broken hearts revealed old and festering wounds that were simultaneously healed. Dormant dreams were awakened and smoldering hopes were fanned into brilliant flame. I watched and listened as a familiar scene from the Bible played itself out—but this time in the prison. Standing on a crudely fashioned stage in regal robes and adored with gold clasps, Pilate said, "...it is your custom for me to release to you one prisoner at the time of the Passover. Do you want me to release 'the king of the Jews'?"

However, in my dream, instead of the actual response, I witnessed throngs of men, women, and children of many races and cultures with raised hands waving palm leaves and purple silk scarves side-to-side, shouted back, "Yes! Jesus. Give us Jesus. Not Barabbas! We want Jesus!"

Yet another dream found me amongst a huddle of people, and like a quarterback hoping to lead his team to victory with this next game strategy, I announced, "God has a marvelously wonderful plan for each of our lives! Now we are going to go out there in the world and live it out to His glory! But first we gonna get our healing on— so that we will be even more effective for God!" I continued with words of encouragement and empowerment that seemed to fly into my mouth like white-winged doves, and out again into the huddle of people. The huddle multiplied in steady streams of people coming from all sections of the stadium like at a Billy Graham crusade.

I prayed, as the sheer number of people responding overwhelmed me, "Lord they are here. What am I to do? I believe enough to lay hands on a few and that you will heal them, but all these?"

I looked toward Heaven, as my arms seem to go liquid, like a special effect from a sci-fi movie. Nothing short of a miracle, I remember thinking in my dream, God you heard me and are answering my prayer. With warm liquid arms, it was not I—but the Lord—who embraced each man, woman, and child. I felt jolts of power surge through my body like being pricked by a thousand pine needles. Then, this power spilled out of these liquid arms, and I watched in awe, as each person's infirmity whether emotional and/or physical was healed. Broken hearts were mended, dreams were resurrected, cancer, AIDS, and everything in between were healed.

I fell on my knees and declared without regard for who heard, "Oh my God, You are real! You have done what You promised...the numbers don't matter to you. Nothing is too hard for you! You are Jehovah-Rophe,

God The Healer. And you heal as many as the grains of sand. Forgive my unbelief."

Even in the dream, I did not feel God's chiding— only a gentle reminder that "With God all things are possible"—whether you believe it or not. God is! It felt more like a kind of reward for my "mustard-seed faith" that spurred me on to the stadium in spite of my feelings of inadequacies.

It seemed that God reminded me, even as I awoke from the dream that it is my great need for Him and humbling myself in that need—that He can be the most effective in and through my life. This willingness, thirst, and readiness to please Him IS what activates the Holy Spirit's empowerment.

As said to Zerubbabel way back in the day, so is said to us today, "...' Not by might nor by power, but by my Spirit,' says the LORD Almighty." (Zechariah 4:6)

Perhaps some of our dreams provide us with more evidence that our hope in God is real, possible, and already playing itself out in the spiritual realm. Perhaps, if we continue to seek His Face in everything and offer our hopes up to Him to be sifted through His Hands, we will be led to God's wonderful and marvelous plans and purposes for our lives. Perhaps, some nights' dreams are a part of God's basic training for the reality of His promises to us that the best is yet to be.

Perhaps, even as we sleep, deep calls to deep to remind us of God's Word hidden in our hearts, "So we fix our eyes not on what is seen, but on what is unseen. For what is seen is temporary, but what is unseen is eternal." 2 Corinthians 4:18

A REFRESHING

Refreshed and my stand steadied, I read this word from the Lord through Marsha Burns' Prophecy Bulletin, this morning, "A special anointing is now being released that will bring regeneration and resurrection power. The tests and trials of the past eight months have taken their toll and have brought a general weakness in your body, soul and spirit. But, now it is time for you to rise up and access this fresh anointing that will refresh, restore and renew. You will do this in the realm of the Spirit by faith. Come boldly, before my throne of Grace, and receive all that I have made available to you, says the Lord."

What hit my spirit as I soaked in this word was regeneration, the activity of spiritual and/or physical renewal. I sure could stand some renewing as the last eight months (at the minimum) have been trying indeed. Lord, knows I am not exaggerating. And I know I'm not the only one. I tell you, a scripture that has kept me moving forward in spite of whatever is going on or not going on is, "For our light and momentary troubles are achieving an eternal glory that far outweighs them all." That one should have an exclamation point on it; but I'm neither to take away nor add to the Word of God.

Moving on, next word that opened up my memory and brought a flood of thanksgiving was resurrection power. I remember God resurrected my life three times, as I lay lifeless in the ambulance after a heroin overdose. The paramedics wouldn't give up and God surely didn't.

He breathed for me when I couldn't breathe for myself. And that was just one incident. Oh, the stories I can tell you. So many near-death experiences, that I can't help but rejoice and know that God has wondrous plans for my life. And one of them is sharing what He's done in and through my life with you, Water-Walker.

Also resurrection brings another reality to mind. Along with my life, slowly but most certainly, God resurrected my dreams. I was without vision for my life. All the things I thought were possible before I tripped over my life slowly faded into the Land of Nevers. My thoughts were dark and hopeless. I'll never write books. I'll never sing. I'll never have a relationship with my son or my parents. I'll never amount to anything. But God blew his cool breath on the smoldering embers once known as hopes and dreams, and He stirred up the fire and fanned the flame into a burning desire to hope again—dream again. Live life more abundantly than ever before.

Rise up is what I feel like when I think about the goodness of the Lord in this here land of the living. Rise up and proclaim! Rise up and declare! Rise up and testify! Rise up and help another child of God rise up! Rise up and walk out my faith! Don't get me started. Too late. Rise up and leap over rainbows taking God at His Word.

Next, restore. Restoration. I've seen it. In my son's eyes when he gives me my medallion at 12-step program anniversary celebrations for many of my 23 years clean and sober. Restoration like when I looked in the mirror and didn't cringe or see dark pools of death anymore; but joy, light and a chocolate-brown-maturing-gracefully beauty smiling back at me. I've tasted it as salty tears when we laid my Dad to rest forever with Jesus; knowing that God gave us years together no longer estranged but a father and daughter who loved and respected one another. That holy kind of restoration I heard and felt when my mom embraced me and said, "Neicy, I love you and I've let it all go. No more resentment for her or for me. I let it all go, too. We flow now, in the love God restored in our hearts.

And so, I come boldly, with arms extended and raised ready to receive all that God preordained for me. And may it be a circle of love as it comes from Him to me, through me to you and from you back to God in thanksgiving and praise.

Refreshed and renewed, my resurrection dance with God continues.

Therefore, having been justified by faith, we have peace with God through our Lord Jesus Christ, through whom also we have access by faith into this grace in which we stand, and rejoice in hope of the glory of God. And not only that, but we also glory in tribulations, knowing that tribulation produces perseverance; and perseverance, character; and character, hope. Now hope does not disappoint, because the love of God has been poured out in our hearts by the Holy Spirit who was given to us. Romans 5:1-5

DEAR HEAVENLY FATHER,

Help us our unbelief. It's not intentional that doubts creep through the cracks and crevices left by disappointments, heartbreaks, betrayals, and the lost-ness that we experienced before You found us. My prayer is neither fancy nor poetic. I simply need You to seal those cracks and crevices with Your love, promises, and Holy touch so that we'll never doubt again. By an act of faith, we choose to believe that You will never leave nor forsake us and that what You promised to do, You will do. Every day, I witness a fraction of the magnitude of who You are and what You do; yet —you call me Your Child and friend. For that, and for You, I am grateful. Amen. So be it!

CHAPTER 9: FAITH TRUSTS

"Let the morning bring me word of your unfailing love,
for I have put my trust in you.
Show me the way I should go,
for to you I lift up my soul."
Psalm 143:8 (NIV)

SPACIOUS PLACE

"He brought me out into a spacious place;
he rescued me because he delighted in me." Psalm 18:19

Oh Lord, look where I am
In such a wide and spacious place
Embraced by Your goodness,
gazing up into Your face.

What joy at the thought of how You've brought me
Braced by Your Hand;
Walking in the Land Of the Living and Plenty
Snatched up from the pit in which I laid hewn
All the baggage and misdeeds behind me lay strewn.

What love You cultivated in my heart
and rooted in my soul
Your miraculous healing touch
and favor render me whole

As I pause and look back for just a minute
You ordered my steps; You're here with me in it.
Had it not been for You on my front, back and side
I would have given up when my faith was really tried

Oh look, Lord, where you brought me!
To this blessed and open space
I feel Your Hands lovingly outlining my face
I'm dancing in your freedom;
Shouting "Hallelujah" in your grace.

GOD SEES WAY DOWN THE ROAD

It all started with my writing a thank-you letter to the CBN *700 Club* in Virginia Beach. I reported how my life had radically changed after watching a dramatization of an ex-addict's life on one of their telecasts. I wrote that I had prayed like he did and asked God to come into my life and live His life through me. I excitedly wrote that I had not used drugs in over sixteen months and that my life was getting better by the day. I also thanked them for paying an old bill, which cleared the way for me to move into my new apartment, as well as referring me to people who gave me furniture for my apartment and clothes to look for a better job—which I got!

As I walked to the mailbox on the corner, I had thoughts of thanksgiving to God for using a television program to reach me with the hope and promise that could be found if I surrendered my life—botches and all—to Him. I had erroneously thought that I had to clean myself up first and then go to God, which is why I probably never sought Him. I never could clean myself up no matter how hard I tried.

I felt glad that God had quickened my heart and mind to write the letter. I walked back to my apartment and went on with the next thing to do in my new faith-walk. I did not give the letter another thought.

Two weeks later, Linda Volcano, a producer from *The 700 Club*, called.

"We received your letter. I'm calling to find out if you are willing to share your story with our viewers."

"For real?"

"Yes, I want to come to Washington with a film crew and shoot a video dramatization of your story. Like the one that you saw that made a difference in your life. We are giving you the opportunity to share with people how it was for you and how a personal relationship with God has changed your life."

"My, my!"

"So, will you? Can we set a date to come up and do this?"

"Yes! Sure! I'd love that!"

We discussed the details. After I hung up the telephone, I immediately picked it up again and dialed my mentor, Dorine.

"Dorine, you won't believe this! *The 700 Club* called me! They want to film a dramatization of my life story."

"Well, all right now! I believe it, baby 'cause you never know what God is gonna do or has in store for us. That's wonderful!"

"But . . . but I'm scared, Dorine. I don't know if I want everyone to know what my life has been like. Plus, they said I have to reenact the drug usage scenes. With syringe and all! But she did say that the syringe would not have needle and that they will use oregano for the marijuana scene. And headache powder or something instead of heroin."

So! There you go. It looks like everything's already been taken care of."

"Yeah, but I will remember. I'll be rolling a pretend joint and have a syringe in my hand. Suppose it will make me want to use drugs again?"

"Then you just go to a twelve-step meeting, let the group know, and it will pass like it has. Where is your faith, Stanice? God is not going to give you such a marvelous opportunity to tell people about what He has done in your life and not take care of you. It's time to put your talk into action. You say you trust Him, right?"

"Yeah!"

"Then, trust Him! You have been prepared for such a time as this. You never know who will see this video and who it will help. That show is seen all across the world. Just help somebody like somebody helped you!"

"Okay, Doe. Thanks. I love you so much."

"I love you, too, baby. It's gonna be all right!"

Several weeks later, Linda and *The 700 Club* film crew arrived. I had asked my son's grandmother to get him out of school early, as there was to be a scene with him and me together in my new faith-walk.

Anyway, the taping went well. The fear left me, as I stayed focused on how God had set this all up way

185

back down the road. I felt like I was relieving it; but the hope I had in the now far outweighed the despair that I had felt in the then. It was like I was asking God to spare me and help me all over again. As I prayed like I had done that day well over a year before, it was like I was praying it for the first time. I forgot all about the cameras surrounding me. It felt like I was relaxing in a semiprivate hot tub filled with the bubbly, steamy waters of peace and pure love.

Somehow, I knew too that this was only the beginning of God's perfect plan for my life.

Several months later, the show aired on New Year's Day. It was part of a telethon called *New Beginnings*. Joy-tears streamed down my cheeks and a multitude of "thank-yous" sprang from my lips as I watched my story on my new nineteen-inch color television in the solitude of my apartment. I couldn't help but think about the goodness, grace, and mercy of such a loving God who saved a wretch like me.

A few weeks following the broadcast, I got another call from *The 700 Club*. They had such a resounding response from people who saw my story and made the decision to surrender their broken lives to God that they wanted me to come to Virginia Beach to do a live interview. So I did that.

In addition to the video and interview, *The 700 Club* included my story in a booklet called *Changed Lives*, and formatted the video into several different languages so it could be viewed in other nations.

In the meantime, I was still so overwhelmed with gratitude that I felt God was leading me to write another letter and mail it in care of *The 700 Club*. However, this letter was to Buddy Baird, the guy whose story I had seen that changed my life.

About two months later, I got another phone call from *The 700 Club*. They wanted me to come back on the show for another live interview. This time I would get a chance to meet Buddy, as we would be interviewed on the show—together!

While all this was going on, God was still working His wonders behind the scenes. Two years after the first airing of my story, I got a call from my ex-husband, CD, whom I had not seen in over twelve years. I didn't even know where he was, if he was alive, and if he was alive I had always wanted the opportunity to ask him to forgive me for the part I played in the breakup of our marriage. And now here he was on the other end of my telephone line.

"Stacey?"

"Yes." Immediately, I knew his baritone voice.

"This is CD, your ex-husband."

"My God, I know! How did you find me? How did you know where I was?"

"My wife and I were looking at *The 700 Club* over a year ago and I saw you. I said, 'Honey, that's Stacey! My ex-wife!'"

I seized the opportunity. "Oh CD, can you ever forgive me for all the hurt I caused you and your family?"

"Stacey, I forgave you a long time ago. I knew you were in trouble even then, but I had no idea it would get so bad for you. I prayed for you, though. Even though I never knew where you were, I always prayed for you because I knew that God knew. And when I saw you on *The 700 Club*, I knew that God had answered my prayers."

"CD," I managed to get out of my throat that was choked with tears.

"It's all right. You just keep doing what you're doing. Somehow, I always knew that you would be all right."

"Thank you, CD."

"Take care, Stacey."

"You too."

"Goodbye."

"Goodbye, CD."

Our vision is so limited. Have you ever left the house a little later than you should have in order to get to an appointment on time? Your anxiety level rises as you check your watch and the traffic slows to a crawl. Then ahead there are the flashing lights of emergency vehicles. A terrible accident comes into view. Suppose you had left on time or a few minutes earlier than you did? Could it have been you being cut out of the mangled car?

Or perhaps you had your mind set on staying at home; but instead you reluctantly consented to go somewhere just to appease that loved one. But by night's end you were really glad that you went. There was something that happened that you would have missed out on if you had stayed at home.

Or perhaps you've taken a job you really didn't want but later you met someone or came across an opportunity that might not have presented itself had you not been on that job.

Or perhaps, like CD, you are praying for someone and as the years slip by your prayers seem futile. CD had no way of knowing where I was physically or spiritually but God knew exactly where I was and what I needed.

Yes, God sees way down the road. He has a plan that encompasses far more than we could ever think or imagine. Plans for the good of not just our individual selves—the me generation that we are—but for all. He loves each of us like we were the only one He has to love—if we only have faith!

BE STILL

Not long ago, my ex-husband called to wish me a Happy Birthday. As we talked I shared with him what was going on in my life. He listened and then offered these simple words, "Be still."

As soon as he said it, the fullness of God's Word sprung up from my heart like a child's abruptly opened jack-in-the-box. "Be still, and know that I am God." (Psalm 46:10). It confirmed for me that God was using my ex-husband to speak His Divine wisdom into my life. That wisdom was carried upon the wings of forgiveness—set up long before the Lord put on this man's heart to call me with the Word.

It was God's love poured into our hearts that enabled us to ask and receive forgiveness from each other and to also forgive ourselves—long ago—which opened the doors wide enough for moments like these.

The next day, during the Feast on THE WORD Gathering in my home, as I shared the testimony of my ex-husband's call, and others present shared their testimonies, the Holy Spirit led us to a prophetic Word. The promise that results once we each determine to "Be still, and know that I am God" in whatever situation we find ourselves.

"You will not have to fight this battle. Take up your positions; stand firm and see the deliverance the LORD will give you, O Judah and Jerusalem. Do not be afraid; do not be discouraged. Go out to face them tomorrow, and the LORD will be with you.' "2 Chronicles 20:17 (NIV)—Personalize it by saying your name.

I believe that what I write here is like a rock thrown by the Holy Spirit into a still, clear lake. It is producing a ripple effect of clarity and promise into our lives today. Receive, partake, feast on THE WORD and be encouraged.

MY SOUL CRIES OUT

Our souls are made up of three parts: mind, will, and emotions. Some days they each are out of kilter with one another. Once I called my mentor, Dorine, to vent my doubts about this, that and the other. She listened and then sympathetically offered, "Stanice, you're okay. Your mind is just not your friend today—that's all."

Our minds try to convince us that we're sinking-that we're not going to make it. Our wills stretch out on us like unruly children in the candy aisle of the supermarket having a conniption fit (as my grandma used to call them) when that can't have what they want exactly when they want it. Even though their loving parents know that what they want will bring them more harm than good.

Our emotions get so jumbled up that we're not sure whether we are stressed, depressed, or plain vexed. It's times like these that we need to come to a screeching halt! And like David shout, *Shut up, my soul* (very loose paraphrase).

In Psalm 116:7, David said, "Be at rest once more, O my soul, for the LORD has been good to you." Again in Psalm 103:2, he instructs his soul, "Praise the LORD, O my soul, and forget not all his benefits."

Like David, we can say, *Mind be at rest!* and replay even a small portion of our testimonies. And ask our minds, *Hasn't God always rescued you—not a moment too soon or too late?*

Will, be at rest! The battle is the Lord's not yours. Hebrews 4:10 reminds us, "For he who has entered His rest has himself also ceased from his works as God did from His." *So, Mind, cease and desist the useless negative chatter, right now, in the Name of Jesus Christ.*

Emotions, be at rest! After all, 2 Corinthians 4:15-17 encourages us, "Therefore we do not lose heart. Though outwardly we are wasting away, yet inwardly we are being renewed day by day. For our light and momentary troubles are achieving for us an eternal glory that far outweighs them all."

Once we start speaking God's Word to our own souls, we will find that we less are dependent on man and more dependent on God—which is a good thing. Man may let us down but God never will.

STANICE ANDERSON

DEAR HEAVENLY FATHER:

Help us to trust You in our everyday living situations. Direct our paths and order our steps toward the plan that you have for our lives. We are grateful for how you provide everything that we need and so many of our wants. We don't know what our future or even the next minute may hold for us; but we are learning that You hold it all. Because You go before us, after us, alongside of us, we have nothing to fear. Strengthen us, encourage us, and give us the hope that we need to move forever forward with our lives. So often, we ask you to do things for us. Well, today, we humbly ask . . . what can we do for you that will encourage someone else's faith-walk? Amen. So be it!

CHAPTER 10: FAITH SOARS

"But those who wait on the LORD
Shall renew their strength;
They shall mount up with wings like eagles,
They shall run and not be weary,
They shall walk and not faint."
Isaiah 40:31 (NIV)

BREATHE DEEP

We are but a breath in the vastness of time.
          So breathe hard,
long,
          and deep
before your future becomes
a once-upon-a-time-long-long-ago-tale
told by generations yet to be conceived.
          Live well.
so that the tale may be sweet smelling incense
          wafting up
          to The Throne Room of God.

              Breath Deep.

              Soar well.

A SEED AND A PRAYER

Looking back, I believe the seed for my second book, *I Say A Prayer For Me: One Woman's Life of Faith and Triumph,* was planted on a cool, dry September evening in 1998. Discouraged and perplexed, I called a childhood friend and confessed, "I poured my heart and soul into the stories I wrote and all I get back are rejection letters from editors saying how powerful my stories. If my stories are so good, why won't the Lord allow magazines to publish them?"

My friend's words were like cool well water on a hot and dusty day. I felt myself refreshed and revived with every word she spoke, so I grabbed a pen and took notes. With authority she spoke and with great abandon I listened:

- "The stories you wrote have not found homes because they ARE a book—it's all one story.

- God WILL use your writing to free people up—but He will use this process to free you up first. You cannot free anyone else until you are free."
  By faith, I received those words as if from the mouth of God. So, I prayerfully typed the notes and filed them away.

In August 1999, I felt led to encourage my friends and began my daily email series, *Food For The Spirit.*

The response? "Why are you sending us other folks' stuff? You are an author now. We want to hear what YOU have to say!"

Although taunted by insecurities, I sat at my computer, prayed and typed, "Show me, Lord." Within a few minutes, my creative juices were flowing and I followed my memories like colorized movies projected on a theater screen. The next day I e-mailed an original life-story to 16 friends.

By the week's end, wonderful responses began pouring in from people all over the world. Seeing how God was using what I wrote fueled me to keep writing.

As the writing of each story neared its' end, it felt like I was dancing in a vast, freshly-cut field. With my head to the sky, I basked in the warmth of God's light as it healed the old and newly broken places in my life and heart. It was like dancing—undisturbed—on Holy Ground.

Then, a need to pray came over me and with eyes closed I heavy-handedly tapped out the prayers on the keyboard. The prayers became a vital part of the story— as did the verses from the Bible. Together they were a kind of adhesive that sealed the freshly written stories.

Soon my son and friends proclaimed, "THESE STORIES that you write ARE your NEXT BOOK!"

"Yeah, sho' you right." My unrelenting insecurities vied to keep the truth from me. But in the stillness of the night, the Lord impressed upon my heart that it was so. This was to be the book that was prophesized through my friend, on a cool, dry and desperate night in September 1998.

COME, WALK ON THE WATER

Today I am reminded by the Holy Spirit to stay focused on Jesus. I am to recognize Him whenever he speaks to my heart, no matter how softly. When I step out of my boat, which I've come to know as my comfort zone; I'm reminded not to look at my circumstances. Though they may be real; they breed fear and apprehension. For God has not given me a spirit of fear but of power, of love, and a sound mind. (1st Timothy...)

"Lord, if it's you," Peter replied, "tell me to come to you on the water."

"Come," he said. Then Peter got down out of the boat, walked on the water and came toward Jesus. But when he saw the wind, he was afraid and, beginning to sink, cried out, "Lord, save me!" Immediately Jesus reached out his hand and caught him. "You of little faith," he said, "why did you doubt?" (Matthew 14:28-31 NIV)

The things that are going on around me in the natural realm don't take into account the spiritual realm and that with God nothing is impossible. My focus is to be on God who is the Author and Finisher of my faith. He is the one that I'm to recognize as I take control of my thoughts so that it is he and he alone that I see, hear, and walk towards.

Let's say that you are walking down a street and you see someone that you believe you know. When your mind recalls that person, you may think, *"Yes, I recognize her or him. That's (name).* You also recognize whether that person is friend or foe and your history with that person.

Well, when we look at Jesus, we too recognize not only who He is but His attributes as well: Ultimate Friend, Savior of the World, Resurrection Power, Love, Mercy, Grace, Lover of our souls, Omnipresent, Lamb of God, and the list goes on. Keeping our eyes focused on Jesus keeps us afloat.

He won't let us sink!

As we step out of our boats, we need to recognize Jesus and keep ours eyes, hearts, minds and spirits glued on Him. At the very moment we do that, we are enabled to walk on the water of God's purpose and calling for our lives. Once we come to believe that we can walk on water, the safety of the *boat* will lose its appeal. We will witness our doubts drowning and find ourselves wholeheartedly following Jesus as He leads us to stilled waters that run deep into our holy destinies.

DISPELLING FEAR

Can you recall a tense situation when fear gripped you by the throat and refused to let you go? Perhaps it was a boss who held up your job like a bone to a dog, insisting that you jump to get it or face firing. Perhaps it was a kid at school who with eyes like small slits and fists raised promised, "This is not over by a long shot. I'll see you after school."

Perhaps on a dark street or lighted underground parking lot when the sound of footsteps not your own were audible from behind; as the person passed, you sighed with relief to find out they were friend and not foe. You Perhaps it was a racially tense moment when you were the only white face in the sea of black faces or vice versa.

As fear's grip tightened, a barely audible and short prayer leapt from deep within your soul straight to the Throne Room of God. Suddenly from somewhere and at predestined defined moment, a supernatural peace enveloped you and with it the courage to face whatever was next.

I believe that nothing comes into our lives that God does not know about and that has not been sifted through His hands.

With God, we have nothing to fear—Ever!

NO MORE FEAR

Fear paralyzed me. Stuck in the middle of an alluding dream going nowhere, I couldn't step back nor could I move forward.

Sick and tired of existing like that, I made a conscious decision—trust God and move forever forward in spite of the fear.

Making that choice revolutionized my life from the inside out.

Oh, yes, I remember the day; I left the *Land of Nevers* at warp speed and headed to where possibilities sifted through God's Hand emerge as High Probabilities. Cradled in a dream, nursed by Hope, and empowered by Faith, I left the safety and predictability of the chicken coup.

Transformed by God,
I took flight and assumed my place
among the eagles.

DISCOVERING THE YOU TO DO

When I complained about being bored one time to Dorine, my mentor, she told me (and once was enough), "Stanice, you're bored because you're boring."

I had to start the search for my new life in Christ and recovery from heroin addiction. I loved to sing in the shower, so I enrolled in music school and took vocal lessons. I sang at 12-step conventions, coffee houses, and at a friend's restaurant in Durham, NC to get over my fear of singing while people watched. I drew a bit, so I enrolled in drawing classes at a community college. I asked a friend to take me to museums and teach me about art. I took public speaking classes at the University of D.C.

During my lunch hours while working at USA TODAY, I went to Toastmasters International sessions where we practiced developing speeches and speaking in front of the group. Another friend gave me a one-day trip book, and we took drove to a different place every other week so I discovered my love for travel.

From there, I began traveling with Dorine to 12-step conventions as she was on the speaker circuit. I considered myself her apprentice; I watched and learned. I even practiced things that other women were teaching me to help me on my quest of becoming a better mother. I tried many things to see what was *me*. Now that I was a born-again Christian, how could any of these interests, talents, or gifts make me available to God and His people?

I enrolled in Honors English classes at a local university to improve my writing. Joined literature and newsletter committees, submitted articles to magazines, and later asked Patrice Gaines, an author and Washington Post reporter, to be my publishing world coach.

My friend, since childhood, Omie Brown, hooked me up with her fellow horse people so I learned how to care for and ride horses. I even took swimming lessons at 40 with 10-year-olds in the shallow end. They encouraged me, "You go, Ms. Stanice, you can do it!" And I, in turn, encouraged them.

This is what I tell people young in the faith or wondering, *What will happen to who I am if I say "Yes to Jesus?*

You will not be bored my friend, sister, or brother in Christ, and you will not be boring. And God will put you with positive and extraordinary folk, if you but ask Him. Christians that are revved up and on-fire-for-Jesus and the ones that aren't you will fuel as they experience your growth, your changing, and what freedom in Christ really looks like. Enthusiasm is contagious. Watch people break out all around you with the purpose and joy of the Lord.

And I'd be remiss if I didn't tell them: "There will be others who will loathe your light but don't take it personally. It's Christ that shines through you—so count it joy."

That's what folk told me. Me who was so bored. Now, there is never a dull moment living for Jesus. So get ready! Buckle up! God is up to something awesome in You and through you!

Just be who you are? Discover who you are in Christ and be it—do you. One thing about people—they can spot a fake! Nobody can do the you that you were born to do.

DEAR HEAVENLY FATHER:

Thank you for going both with me and before me. Thank you that there is no place that we can possibly go; where You are not there too. Thank You for the gift of friendship and the people that You place in our lives that walk out Your love and care for us. So today, I confess my doubts, for only in confessing where I really am can You move me forward to where I really need to be. Although I don't know what's around the bend, I know The One who is The Maker of Bends and everything else I can see—and don't see.

Your love and care for us is truly amazing. As we learn to walk by faith and not by sight, thank You for allowing us to take toddler steps toward You until we get our bearings and learn to walk, run, and soar with wings like eagles. Continue to teach us your ways all the days of our lives.

Show me the genuine self you created me to be. Use me and all that I am in You, to bless the world. Take me further in You until I discover like Abraham discovered that you are indeed Jehovah-Jireh, God my provider. Amen. So be it!

COMPELLED TO WRITE

I've been writing since I learned how to construct a sentence. One of my poems was published in school magazine when I was nine years old. It seemed like, in the millisecond, my happy childhood ended, as the verbal and physical abuse at home escalated. Coupled with being raped at 14 years old, I was emotionally silenced and sequestered by the secrets. I remember making a vow to myself—"No one must ever know." Therefore, the written word became my saving-grace.

As I grew older, I attempted to show the world a well-adjusted, funny, and extraverted woman. It was only in my writing that my real voice could be heard. It dared to whisper a different story. Words befriended me, flowed from my soul, and spilled onto thousands of pages over the years. However, as if by tried by a jury with my warped sense of self as foreman, most of my pieces were sentenced to life in file folders neatly stacked in corrugated boxes and exiled to the backside of closets.

Resurrected Dreams, one of the stories in my memoir, *I Say a Prayer For Me: One Woman's Life of Faith and Triumph*, best describes my relationship with the written word.

♫ *Out came the sun and dried up all the rain.* ♫

In my forties, writing found me again. It helped shatter the chains of my painful and shameful past. Words fed my starving spirit and soothed my aching life. In spite of the fact that I abandoned the words and left them to die by the side of the road, they waited for me at the crossroads of life to point the way, 'Just believe!' they insisted that we and you are one.'

♫ *The itsy bitsy spider went up the spout again.* ♫

As an exercise of my belief, I send my words out into the world.

Yes, I am compelled to write.

I am compelled to encourage.

I am compelled to love.

I am compelled to walk on water when the ground ain't enuf.

Let's walk on the water, you and I.

Come on! Get your faith wet.

DEAR HEAVENLY FATHER:

Give us the progressive vision that You have for our lives. Protect our minds against the invasion of negative and nonproductive thoughts that seek to defeat us. When the harshness of life seems to wash us out, remind us to get up and look up to You. Help us to inch our way back up the spout again and claim Your victory with every step we take. Thank you that our lives do have meaning and purpose! Breathe life into our dry bones and fan the flames under our smoldering dreams. Help us to believe that it's never too late to follow that dream and vision for our lives. Order our steps and how us that we can do all things with You as our Helper. Thank you for creating talents and gifts within us that we may use them to your glory. Amen. So be it!

Having then gifts differing according to the grace that is given to us, let us use them: if prophecy, let us prophesy in proportion to our faith; or ministry, let us use it in our ministering; he who teaches, in teaching; he who exhorts, in exhortation; he who gives, with liberality; he who leads, with diligence; he who shows mercy, with cheerfulness.
Romans 12:6-8 (New King James Version)

AFTER WORDS

- Acknowledgements

- The WOW Zone Experience

- The WOW Zone Project

- Reader Groups

- Reflection and Discussion Guide

ACKNOWLEDGEMENTS

First and foremost, I thank God for providing absolutely everything I needed to write, print, distribute, and promote this book; including my son, Mike Tucker, Jr., and my mother, Virginia Anderson, who by choice and by faith launched out into the deep waters, stepped out of the boat, and walked on water with me in producing this first book in *The WOW Zone™ Series*, **WALKING ON WATER WHEN THE GROUND AIN'T ENUF**.

Thank you gifted editorial team, headed by Executive Editor, Mike E. Tucker Jr. When I called out for help, you answered expediently and generously. Lee Ivory, Kareema Cockrell, Beverly Mahone, Merrill Jones, Jacci Wordsmith, Rebecca Bishophall, Jennifer Ashton, Rhonda Monroe, Delphine Glaze, Lynn McGee, Cynthia Battle, Cam Poles, and an anonymous author.

Thank you DaMaris Hill for writing the **REFLECTION AND DISCUSSION GUIDE** included in this edition. Thank you Demont Peekaso Pinder for the oil painting and Denise Johnson for the graphics. You used your tremendous talents to translate my vision into the stellar art that adorns this book.

Thank you Feast on The Word Gathering and Fellowship family: Omie Brown, Peggy Stroman, Trayce Traynham, Pam Turner, Carol Ayo Durodola, Lois McFarland, Cindy Jett, Cassandra Saunders, and DaMaris Hill for your prayers, guidance, and support.

ACKNOWLEDGEMENTS

Thank you **WOW ZONE™ TEAM**: Joyce Burnette, Keisha Hooks, Claudia Holloway, Sharon Hockaday, Onyango Sawyer, John Austin, Pam Lockhart, Sharon Lynn Couch, Brenda Garard, Barbara Turner, Randy Jones, Thelma Harris, Donna Bexley, Carla Watson, Shirley Stewart, Nicole Davis, Leland Caraway, District 51 and my Anderson, Somerville, and Alexander families.

Thank you author friends who pray, counsel, and challenge me through your writing to strive for excellence; including Marilynn Griffith, Claudia Mair Burney, Sharon Ewell Foster, Sonnie Beverly, Victoria Christopher Murray, Jacquelin Thomas, Melodie Kent, Sonnie Beverly, Barbara Joe Williams, Michele Andrea Brown, Terrie Williams and Patrice Gaines.

Thank you my exquisite grandchildren. You are the warm trade winds beneath my water wings! Michal Zoe, our budding artist, your design suggestions for the chapter title pages made this book better than it would have been without you. Arin, Nya Jo and Michal Zoe, you passed the question, "Grandma, are you through with your book yet?" like a baton between Olympian athletes pressing toward the finish line. You helped me with your promise of rewards that awaited me upon completion. I love you! You are Grandma's rewards!

Thank you Dorine Phelps and all my *anonymous* friends. Your unconditional love, friendship and counsel, through the years, helped revolutionize my life.

My reader friends, I am totally grateful for you. Many of you have been with me since my Food for the Spirit and other email series and before my first published book. You've been incredibly loyal, kind, encouraging, and supportive. You've shared my works with others, supported my events and one-woman shows, as well as recommended me as an inspirational speaker to your organizations.

Some of you, I've met in my travels; some, I pray that God will allow us to meet someday. Bottom line, all of us have met spirit-to-spirit, heart-to-heart, within the pages and the prayers. I am a better writer, perhaps even a better woman because of our interaction. Thank you.

As a postscript: On the evening that I finished the book, my six-year-old granddaughter, Michal Zoe, presented me with an award certificate with hand-drawn green, yellow, and purple stars, that reads: **AWARD** – good job for finishing Your Book!11/9/10

DEAR HEAVENLY FATHER,

Thank you for keeping your promises to me and meeting each reader within the words and breathing hope, love, healing, peace, laughter, and amazing unshakable faith into their life. Special blessings to all who help me along the way. For all of the people, I've mentioned and those I inadvertently forgot to mention, and those whose paths you will allow mine to cross, I ask you to bless them with the most fervent desires of their hearts. Please heap into their lives blessings and saturate their lives, as well as the lives of those they touch, with unprecedented favor. In Your Son's Matchless Name, I pray. Amen. So be it!

THE WOW ZONE EXPERIENCE

Water-Walkers, we invite you to continue your experience with **WOW ZONE™** experience on our website at:

TRYWALKINGONWATER.COM

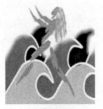

- Share how God met you within the pages and read what others are saying about how they were met.

- Read Stanice's blog and events' calendar.

- Purchase custom signed bookplates, the E-book and paperback copies of **WALKING ON WATER WHEN THE GROUND AIN'T ENUF.**

- Find out how you can participate in **THE WOW PROJECT** that gets books into the hands of people experiencing difficult times.

- Sign up for **THE WOW ZONE™** newsletter and read the latest news on **THE WOW PROJECT.**

- Tap into hundreds of 12-step and other spiritual resource links compiled by the author.

- Purchase CDs, DVDs, and other **WOW ZONE™ WATER-WALKER** products.

For information on booking Stanice Anderson as speaker, workshop facilitator, and/or performance artist, contact booking@TryWalkingOnWater.com.

THE WOW PROJECT

Against all odds and exercising our water-walking faith, let's help usher **WALKING ON WATER WHEN THE GROUND AIN'T ENUF** onto *The New York Times* and every other bestseller list in the country. This is most important because we want this book in the hands people who are experiencing difficult times and need to be inspired, encouraged and infused with hope to know that they can get through everything and overcome anything with water-walking faith in God.

Long before I completed my manuscript for my second book, **I SAY A PRAYER FOR ME**, God promised me that He would meet each reader within the pages. God has been faithful, as evidenced by countless, emails and conversations with readers from around the globe. "He is the same yesterday, today, and forever" and so are His promises.

If you'd like to seize opportunities to share this book with others, then consider **THE WALKING ON WATER PROJECT**; simply called:

THE WOW PROJECT

If God met you within the pages and you were moved by the message of this book, you probably already have some exceptional ideas as to how to best let others know about it. Here are some ideas to help you share this book with others:

Give the book to friends, co-workers, family members, even strangers, as a gift. They not only get gripping and entertaining real life stories, monologues, poetry and stuff like that; but a glimpse into the personal and intimate relationship with God that is possible where you come to know that you know that you know: God cares about absolutely every detail of your life.

Leave an extra copy on your church pew, on the train, in a cab. Drop off a few copies in the hospital waiting areas, your doctor's office, and anywhere a word of hope and encouragement would be welcomed.

Buy a set of books as gifts to battered women's shelters, prisons, homeless and transitional shelters, or domestic violence safe houses, detoxification centers, drug treatment centers, church ministries, group homes, youth programs, and other places where its' message would be appreciated and lives could be changed. We also offer volume discount pricing for orders of ten (10) books or more. Contact sales@TryWalkingOnWater.com.

Share it through your social network sites, including, FaceBook.com, Twitter.com, LinkedIn.com, etc.

➤ Write a book review for your favorite magazines, local newspaper, organization newsletter, or websites that you frequent. Write one, save it, and you can cut and paste it onto many different media.

➤ Ask your favorite radio shows or podcasts to have the author on as a guest. Often, media people give more attention to listeners' requests than to publicists' press releases.

➤ Do you have a business, shop or store? Consider displaying books on your counter to resell to customers. Books are available at a discounted rate on our website www.TryWalkingOnWater.com and by sending email to sales@TryWalkingOnWater.com.

➤ Talk about the book on e-lists or other forums. Don't make it an advertisement; but, rather share your experience with the book. How it impacted your life along with a link to **THE WOW ZONE™** website, **WWW.TRYWALKINGONWATER.COM**.

➤ Purchase books to give as premium gifts for new membership, customer level attainments, or employee incentives.

➤ When assembling care packages for people in need of a hand-up, consider adding copies of **WALKING ON WATER WHEN THE GROUND AIN'T ENUF**.

For more up-to-date information and ideas on how you can seize opportunities to help spread this message of hope found in water-walking faith, check out **THE WOW PROJECT** on our web site at TryWalkingOnWater.com.

THE WOW PROJECT

READER GROUPS

INVITE STANICE TO YOUR BOOK CLUB MEETING
Stanice Anderson enjoys in-person visits with book clubs and other reader groups to discuss her books. To book Stanice for an in-person book discussion for a modest honorarium, contact booking@TryWalkingOnWater.com.

BOOK SPEAKERPHONE CHATS WITH STANICE
Stanice offers 30-minute phone chats with book clubs, women's ministries and bookstores around the country. To arrange a Speakerphone Chat for your group or bookstore, email booking@TryWalkingOnWater.com. "In-Depth Chat" over 30 minutes, also available.

BOOK VIRTUAL VISITS WITH VIA SKYPE™
Would you like Stanice to talk to your class, library, book club, women's ministry, or bookstore? Set up a virtual author visit with her via Skype™ streaming live video. Stanice offers "Meet the Author" 10-15-minute visits. "In-Depth Author Visit" for 20-40 minutes are also available. Use contact form on Stanice's website at www.TryWalkingOnWater.com or send email to booking@TryWalkingOnWater.com.

ORDER WOW ZONE™ WATER-WALKER KITS
Stanice is offering a **WALKING ON WATER READER GROUP KIT** that features autographed bookplates and custom bookmarks to encourage the **WATER-WALKER** in you. She can also include a 30-minute speakerphone chat or 15-minute Skype™ virtual visit on the day of your group's party or at another agreed upon time.

For details, visit **www.TryWalkingOnWater.com** or email WaterWalker@TryWalkingOnWater.com.

CONSIDER HAVING A WATER-WALKER PARTY Stanice Anderson believes that after reading this book, you'll be inspired to write and share your own water-walker stories, testimonies, spokentry, and monologues. Hopefully, you will want to host a **WALKING ON WATER WHEN THE GROUND AIN'T ENUF PARTY** to include pieces written by group members.

Consider inviting your family and friends. Also consider inviting Stanice Anderson for a virtual visit via Skype™ for a fun and unique interactive experience. She can read and/or perform a few pieces from the books.

REFLECTION AND DISCUSSION GUIDE
BY DaMARIS HILL

CHAPTER ONE: FAITH TESTIFIES

"And they overcame him by the blood of the Lamb, and by the word of their testimony..." Revelation 12:11 (NIV)

The enemy of our souls attempts to steal, kill, and destroy God's hope for us. This negativity shows up in many ways. Some of us find ourselves easily aggravated by a neighbor or co-worker. Some of us doubt our abilities, while others invite or maintain negative relationships.

Consider your life a daily walk with God. What are some challenges you would like to overcome? What are some positive spiritual habits that you can introduce into your lifestyle that will help you overcome? Pray and ask God for help. Believe that He will provide you with the strength and everything else you may need to overcome.

CHAPTER TWO: FAITH PURIFIES

"When you pass through the waters, I will be with you; and when you pass through the rivers, they will not sweep over you. When you walk through the fire, you will not be burned; the flames will not set you ablaze." Isaiah 43:2 (NIV)

Faith is a difficult thing to manage, especially when it is sandwiched between Heaven and our earthly desires. Other times our desires are so appealing, in faith, we fix and squint our eyes to make our desires look like what God must want for our lives. We convince ourselves that God wants what we want. What desires do you have that have wedged their way between you and your faith?

Before Stanice does anything, she prays a simple prayer, "Lord, show me." That's her way of actively inviting God into the process. God loves such invitations and as you've seen through her testimonies, He responds in wonderful and astounding ways.

CHAPTER THREE: FAITH REMEMBERS

"God works all things together for the good of those who love Him and are called according to His purposes." Romans 8:28 (NIV)

Take a few moments. Write a letter to yourself. Remind yourself of your divine purpose. If you are unsure, open your heart and ask God to guide your letter. Keep this letter. Read it when you are discouraged. Read it and be reminded of God's will for your life. Be encouraged. Despite your trials—all things work together for the good of God

CHAPTER FOUR: FAITH LAUGHS

"Do not grieve, for the joy of the LORD is your strength." Nehemiah 8:10 (NIV)

What are the joys that lie in the details of your life? Tell a funny story to a friend. Share some joy.

CHAPTER FIVE: FAITH HOLDS ON

"Perseverance must finish its work so that you may be mature and complete, not lacking anything." James 1:4 (NIV)

Consider the trials in your life. Have there been obstacles in your life journey that seemed unbearable? Have they strengthened you? Have they strengthened your spiritual life? Make a three column list. On the left column, write your challenges and obstacles. In the center column, write what aspect of your life or spiritual journey has been strengthened as a result of that obstacle. In the right column, write the greatest possibility that can come as a result of this challenge. If you are not sure what to write in the far right column, leave it blank. Fill it in when God reveals the *wait-blessing* to you.

CHAPTER SIX: FAITH LETS GO

"Do not be anxious about anything, but in everything, by prayer and petition, with thanksgiving, present your requests to God. And the peace of God, which transcends all understanding, will guard your hearts and your minds in Christ Jesus." Philippians 4:6-7 (NIV)

Letting go is never easy, because it involves change and change can be difficult in any capacity. When you doubt if you should let go, ask yourself, "anxiety or peace?" Let go of anything that refuses to let peace flourish in your life. God does not want you to live in fear. Pray and ask him for help.

Remind yourself what peace is. Write a little about a peaceful moment that you enjoyed alone or shared with someone else. Activities can also introduce peace into your life. Try spending a few moments with a hobby like painting or playing music each day or something you like to do but rarely make time to do it; i.e., go to a museum, take a cooking class, go for a walk at sunset.

CHAPTER SEVEN: FAITH HOPES

"God says, I alone know the plans I have for your life; plans for prosperity and not disaster, plans to give you a future and a hope". Jeremiah 29:11-14 (NIV)

What do you do well? Let your talents and abilities serve as sparks of hope for prosperity. Sometimes others see you better than you see yourself. Begin to live in your answered prayers. Make a plan today. How can your talents and abilities lead to your personal growth and prosperity?

CHAPTER EIGHT: FAITH BELIEVES

"But without faith it is impossible to please Him, for he who comes to God must believe that He is, And that He is a rewarder of those who diligently seek Him." Hebrews 11:6 (NKJV)

Believe in yourself. Look in the mirror. Notice God's beauty within you. Where is God's beauty recognizable in your life? And where do you seek God? In what spaces is your relationship with God strongest? Embrace your beauty and believe it can be used to bless the world. Ask God to begin to reveal the wonderful plans He has for your life.

CHAPTER NINE: FAITH TRUSTS

"Let the morning bring me word of your unfailing love, for I have put my trust in you. Show me the way I should go, for to you I lift up my soul." Psalm 143:8 (NIV)

Choose three issues that you are going to trust God about. Pray that these issues are in the will of God and not exclusive to your mind, will, and emotions. Write the three issues down and post them on your refrigerator or calendar. Each time God strengthens your faith in these three areas, write it down and post. We learned earlier that the enemy will try to destroy us using negative thoughts and Whispers of Doubt. Keep a record of acts of your faith as a reminder of God's grace.

CHAPTER TEN: FAITH SOARS

"But those who wait on the LORD Shall renew their strength; They shall mount up with wings like eagles, They shall run and not be weary, They shall walk and not faint." Isaiah 40:31 (NIV)

God's plans will always exceed your expectations. Jesus asked God to teach him how to pray. God answered with the Lord's Prayer. Like Jesus, you can ask God to reveal the plans He has for your life and show you how to live in His will. Ask God to show you how to walk on water. Begin tracking your journey. Write it down and/or verbally share your testimony with others. Like Stanice Anderson, charting your journey toward unwavering and water-walking faith can provide encouragement and hope for others.

227

Sign up for Stanice Anderson's **WOW Zone Newsletter** for inspiration, updates, products, giveaways, speaking events, book signings in your area, and information about more books in the WOW Zone Series.

WWW.TRYWALKINGONWATER.COM

LaVergne, TN USA
09 December 2010
208065LV00001B/7/P